A Common Mission

A Common Mission

Healthy Patterns in Congregational
Mission Partnerships

DAVID WESLEY

FOREWORD BY
ROBERT J. PRIEST

RESOURCE *Publications* · Eugene, Oregon

Contents

Foreword by Robert J. Priest | vii

Preface | xi

Acknowledgments | xv

1   A Grass Roots Phenomenon | 1
2   A Shared Mission | 17   —> 1. common agenda
3   A Reciprocal Mission | 35   —> 2. reciprocity
4   Communicating the Mission | 57   —> 3. clear communication
5   The Church as Missionary | 70   —> God's mission
6   Collective Impact | 88
7   A Common Mission | 104

Bibliography | 113

An Invitation to Partnership | 117

Foreword

By Robert J. Priest

THIS BOOK BY DAVID Wesley focuses on new patterns of American global mission involvement, new patterns that are only just beginning to be better understood. And this book, based on careful research, provides an outstanding overview of the new ways in which global missionary involvements are increasingly taking place. Anyone wishing to understand and wisely consider Christian mission in the contemporary world needs to read this book.

In earlier eras the pattern of Christian missionary activity looked rather different than it does today. Travel was slow, requiring days, weeks, or even months for missionaries to arrive at their destinations. Furthermore, travelers were less able to count on finding numerous English speakers in destination sites, requiring missionaries to go through a long period of language and culture learning if they were to be able to communicate at all. And again in earlier eras missionaries were often doing pioneering work, where there was no mature body of local churches and well-trained Christian leaders to partner with and count on for the central task of verbally commending the gospel to others.

All of this meant that the task of Christian mission required trained career professionals who would invest a great deal of time to acquiring linguistic fluency and cultural understanding, as well as theological training, for specialized long-term service.

This also required the creation of specialized mission agencies and boards that would take primary responsibility for supervising and directing the mission work on the various fields. Because travel and communication was slow, supporting churches in America or Europe were understood as unable to provide close oversight of field missionaries, and they lacked the contextual knowledge of destination sites necessary for wise oversight. The role of sending churches then was limited to vetting, financially supporting, and praying for career missionaries and mission agencies or boards.

The world today is rather different. Communication worldwide is instant. Travelers can arrive almost anywhere on earth within a day or two. This means that travelers can use short windows of vacation time to travel and serve. And when they arrive, they can always find local people who speak their language. Large swaths of the globe, such as Swaziland, which used to have few Christians or churches now have many large and vibrant churches. The need in many such places is less for career missionaries who will laboriously learn another language and spend their lives doing the pioneer work of initially communicating the gospel and planting churches, but for partnering relations that will keep the ministry of local Christians at the center. Today, the divide between America, say, and a country like Swaziland is not a divide between a place that has churches and the gospel and a place that does not, but rather is a divide between places that each have churches, but where in one place the churches and Christian institutions are older and more established within an economic order that is strong, and another place where the churches are new and growing, but within contexts of great financial and material constraint.

Christian ministries have always required material underpinnings that allow pastors to be supported, church buildings to be provided, educational structures for leaders to be trained, and ministry and service structures that serve the wider world. And the material context in which American Christians operate is quite different from the material context in which Christians operate in much of the world. This affects everything from the amount and quality of education that people routinely are able to acquire in a given country, to the amount and kind of resources that church members are able to give. It also affects the wider pattern of human need that churches are called on to serve. In Swaziland poverty creates both opportunities for ministry and constraints on ministry. But when churches in America and Swaziland partner together on significant needs and ministries in Swaziland, they take advantage of the respective strengths of each partner in the context of strategic ministry opportunities in ways that either partner, alone, would be poorly positioned to address.

Today communication is instant and travel rapid. This means that church members and church leaders in America can travel back and forth to Swaziland using short blocks of time, such as in a brief vacation, and can coordinate plans through instant communication. They can partner in destination sites with large numbers of Christian leaders who already speak their language. Since this does not involve supervision of large numbers of career missionaries, American Christians and their churches see less need for a separate mission agency or denominational board to control and supervise the process, but instead directly enter into partnering relations with churches and other institutions in destination sites. That is, larger US congregations take a more central role in all aspects of missionary partnerships, and create new positions for mission pastors to help coordinate the process, and field brokers to represent them in field settings. Such congregations mobilize their networks of relational and cultural and material resources to help accomplish strategic ends in distant places.

In this important book David Wesley helps us understand these new contours of global ministry that increasingly characterize American global mission involvements. He points out some of the characteristic weaknesses and challenges that such ministry partnerships need to overcome, as well as the strengths involved in such approaches, given the nature of our contemporary world. And he provides wise advice for everyone involved in such partnerships.

Preface

CONTRIBUTORS TO THIS BOOK include nearly 200 individuals interviewed in the countries of Botswana, Lesotho, Namibia, South Africa, Swaziland, and the United States. The research process involved data collected and analyzed against other research in the same area.

A desire for meaningful relationships, as well as an aspiration to effectively help others, wove its way into nearly every interview. Like young couples in love, people passionately shared pictures and stories of friends across the world. Individuals kindled relationships as they shared their common bond in God's mission. Unsurprisingly, challenges also surfaced common to any developing relationship. Although people entered partnership with hopes of doing good, there were times when good intentions had damaging consequences for the recipients of the good will.

Repeatedly people responded to the question why they would take risks and sacrifice as they did. Their comments did not revolve around terms of obligation or duty. Rather their reactions were those of relationship and love. Women in Swaziland sacrificially cared for their neighbors dying of AIDS. Women and men in the U.S. sold cars, petitioned work colleagues, and organized events to raise money. Christians in Africa shared their children's clothes and food with orphans, and pastors in the U.S. as well as Africa told of renewal within their congregation as a result of partnerships.

This book does not contain a "one size fits all" program. Practical patterns for healthy partnerships, however, surfaced through the research process. Patterns surfaced in large churches of 7000 or more people akin to similar patterns in smaller churches of 50-150 people. Ultimately five common patterns emerged from the research, patterns that guide healthy partnerships. These patterns form the framework for Common Mission.

These principles will prove helpful to churches learning how to have healthy, cross-cultural partnerships. Pastors and ministerial students should also find this book informative as they lead congregations in mission.

The stories that people shared with me provided a description of faithful partnerships and healthy patterns. I also utilized some theological and missiological terms to give a more precise interpretation to my findings. I realize that some terms may not be familiar to all who would read this book. The following short glossary serves as a point of reference for some of these terms. Note each brief description of terms really represents often more complex, extensive descriptions. These short descriptions merely give the reader a point of reference as they read. Further study can be done on any of these terms through a search in theological and missiological dictionaries.

Ecclesiology: Ecclesiology refers to the disciplined theological study of the church. Theologians and ministers often use the term in place of the word "church," simply because people associate church with a building or denominational structure. While the building and structure prove essential, ecclesiology goes beyond this concept to an understanding of the church as the body of Christ, a community that continually assembles and is sent by God.

Paternalism: Paternalism describes the practice of dealing with others as a parent dealing with children. This perspective can be seen through excessive benevolence, or through undue control in relationships. Readers will find the terms paternalism and dependency often used together in many places in this book since paternalistic practices lead to dependency instead of independence. Paternalism remains a temptation and challenge for partnerships in which churches with resources desire to be benevolent toward their partners with limited resources. This book describes how these practices often lead to a lack of trust and lack of acknowledgement of resources beyond financial resources.

Colonialism: Colonialism normally refers to foreign occupation and control of a location. Missiologists often use this interpretive term to describe missionaries who imposed values and practices of their home culture on the location where they served. A major contribution within the field of missiology in the past century entailed identifying and addressing unhealthy colonialist practices. For the purposes of this book, colonialism emerges as U.S. congregations disregard the values and strengths of partner congregations in locations such as Africa. It should be noted that colonialism normally comes from those who have good intentions, but insist on working from their own cultural framework. The book provides several examples of this tendency.

Missionary Ecclesiology: The term missionary ecclesiology in this book describes the mission nature of the whole church as opposed to isolated mission programs. Beyond this general definition, the term provides an acknowledgement that theology and mission prove inseparable. Mission practice must be undergirded by theological understanding. Likewise theology cannot be separated from mission practice.

Ecumenism/Ecumenic: This term describes mission conferences of the 20th century among Christians from a variety of denominations. Although those who attended the conferences came from diverse theological traditions, they found common ground in the historic Christian confessions and particularly in God's mission.

Reciprocity: The term "reciprocity" represents a foundational element within the healthy patterns found in this book. The term refers to an exchange or interaction with others for mutual benefit. This assumes that within partnerships, both parties have something to teach, or contribute. It also assumes that both parties have something to learn or receive.

Acknowledgments

THE RESEARCH AND WRITING of this book reflects the theme of the book. Every stage has been a shared effort. I am grateful to the nearly 200 people in various countries who have graciously allowed me access to their lives, homes and tables. They have taken time to tell me their story and share insight during the research process. I am especially grateful to Filimao Chambo and David Busic who open the doors for me in Swaziland and at Bethany First Church. During my research at Bethany First Church Barbi Moore made sure that I had access to the people and information that I needed. In Swaziland Colleen Copple, Evan and Andrea Mosshart, Jimmy and Brenda Haines and Carriot and Evelyn Shongwe were great hosts. The meals and fellowship shared with Samuel Hynd on Sunday afternoons in Manzini was a gift that I cherish. In the U.S. people from churches in partnership took time for early morning and lunch meetings, they gave me access to their leaders who shared their passion for mission. Beyond this several key people and organizations have encouraged me or provided grants that allowed me to complete research and move the research into writing. These include the Africa Regional Office for the Church of the Nazarene, SAI International/Servant Forge, and Global Mission. Trinity Evangelical Divinity School, notably Craig Ott and Robert Priest gave valuable direction during my dissertation process and encouraged me to move my research toward writing beyond my dissertation. My colleague at Nazarene Theological Seminary,

Acknowledgments

Dean Blevins amongst others gave valuable input into shortening sentences that seemed to go on for several pages, cleaned up the multitude of indirect verbs, and asked clarifying questions that have made this manuscript more accessible. Matt Price, Dennis Albertson and Norm Henry took time to read the final manuscript and give input that led to last minute revisions. Finally I would like to thank Glynda who always helps me see the big picture and not get lost in the forest of abstract thinking. In short, I am blessed. My life and work is enriched by this journey that we take together.

1

A Grass Roots Phenomenon

*"Every few hundred years in Western history there occurs a
sharp transformation . . . within a few short decades, society
rearranges itself – its worldview, its basic values, its social and
political structures, its arts, its key institutions. Fifty years
later, there is a new world. And the people born then cannot
even imagine the world in which their grandparents lived,
and into which their own parents were born. We are currently
living through just such a transformation"*

—PETER DRUCKER, POST-CAPITALIST SOCIETY[1]

THE TERM *UBUNTU* ARTICULATES an African understanding of our
need to connect to one another in order to be complete. Likewise
the title *A Common Mission* offers a description of churches that
connect with one another through the growing phenomenon of
mission partnerships. The word "common" indicates something
shared amongst equals. The word common also suggests something present in all parts of an organism, production, or narrative,

1. Drucker, *Post-Capitalist Society*, 1993, 1

such as a common thread. These two aspects of commonality provide an important orientation for contemporary mission. Mission efforts in the midst of a changing global context are challenging. The signposts of the past century prove difficult, if not impossible to navigate mission efforts into the future.

Since 2008, congregational partnerships emerged so quickly and spontaneously that very few researchers originally noticed this groundswell. Still, partnerships remain present in over 80 percent of United States mega-churches, and prominent in a large number of smaller U.S. churches. In 2008, I heard anecdotal stories about partnerships. The narratives resulted in my addressing the subject for my doctoral dissertation. Through this process I listened to stories from Christians in Swaziland, South Africa, and the United States. People from differently sized churches talked about partnerships formed between congregations in different parts of the globe. Research conversations about partnerships occurred in coffee shops, walking down the beaten paths of Africa, in homes, and under spreading shade trees. They occurred in places of worship and nearly anywhere people would agree to talk to me. In the process, I heard passionate stories that describe an emerging pattern of mission engagement.

In 2012, I met an engineer named Fred at a Panera restaurant in Oklahoma City. He told me that his involvement in his church's partnership brought his whole life into focus. As we met, he spread pictures from his trips across the table. One picture he singled out revealed a ten year old African boy drinking water from a blue plastic cup as a drop of the water fell from the boy's chin. Fred became emotional as he told me this picture demonstrated how the partnership allowed him to experience the greatness of God. Fred described how God led him to build a friendship with Jimmy Braithwaite, a South African who owned a pump company in Swaziland. Jimmy developed the plans for a low maintenance solar paneled water pump that Fred's church could install. The community where the boy lived lacked clean drinking water; however, the new water pump gave them access to water that they did not previously have. Fred then said, "the rest of this story is about how

God multiplied water just like he multiplied bread and fish." From the patent designed for this first well, and the network of people involved in the partnership, a five million dollar grant resulted in similar solar paneled water wells throughout Swaziland. Two years later, the water system received two global awards totaling over 50 million dollars. The awards provided the establishment of similar wells throughout Sub Sahara Africa. The friendship between Fred and Jimmy was the catalyst to network a system that is impacting thousands of lives throughout Africa.

Since 2008, I have heard similar stories where people found a sense of fulfillment and passion as they engaged in congregational partnerships. On a trip to Africa, I met a medical doctor donating a portable X-ray machine that cost nearly $70,000. After training those who would use the equipment in rural communities, the doctor watched with satisfaction as an eight-year-old Swazi girl, just diagnosed with HIV/AIDS, became the first person to benefit from his gift. This girl, like many others, received much improved treatment as doctors could document and follow her development. On several occasions, I heard pastors talk about how a central focus on mission brought a sense of renewal and purpose to their congregations. In Africa, I witnessed Christians faithfully living their faith in the face of overwhelming circumstances. I heard those in Africa tell me that the partnership allowed them to minister in greater ways as they worked alongside their guest partners. Many of those in Africa stated these partnerships gave their churches credibility as they met community needs of clean water and improved health.

Of course, some aspects of these partnerships prove healthier than others, and some congregations remain more intentional than others. After the interviews and findings from over 200 people in numerous locations, I began to find some common threads, or best practices that appear consistent throughout the variety of locations and partnerships. These practices form the framework of this book.

THE EMERGENCE OF PARTNERSHIPS IN THE MIDST OF GLOBAL INSTABILITY

The 21st century church lives in a time of unprecedented global challenge and transition. Many congregations chose not to retrench resources, or withdraw from their commitment to missions, during these financial challenges and changing global dynamics. Instead, churches find innovative ways to multiply their mission involvement and financial commitments. This growth includes more than simply supporting missionary causes. As congregations seek to live into God's mission within a shifting global context, they also find new patterns for mission engagement. Although this movement carries a risk of destructive dependency and paternalism, it represents a greater potential for unprecedented mission opportunities.

These shifts in missions corresponded to a shift in globalization, one described by Robert Schreiter as Third Wave Mission. Schreiter defined the first wave of mission as the movement occurring during the time when missionaries accompanied explorers and traders. Primarily Jesuits, these missionaries traveled at the request of the monarch. The second wave, according to Schreiter, began early in the 19th century with the formation of many mission agencies and denominations. During this period of many global and political changes, missions served as means to expand the church throughout the world. Also, during this time, critics challenged missionary movements because of their organizations' link to colonialization.

Third wave mission, according to Schreiter, occurs within a third wave of globalization. The movement began in the 1990s and continues today. Third wave of globalization results in a dramatic compression of space and time. Information about distant events appears instantly available. Journeys that used to take months, weeks or days occur in a few hours. Schreiter argues this compression raises the question of what the term "mission field" now means. He writes, "Deterritorialization . . . elements of culture now float around free of their original locations . . . Territory and national culture are thus increasingly not boundary markers for mission and mission society-identity." Within this globalization movement, the missionary's focus shifts from lifelong mission commitments toward shorter-term commitments. Lastly, the third wave of globalization blurs or erases the exotic differences of people in far off lands. Third wave mission exists as a response to third wave globalization. The shift includes the emergence of lay involvement, short-term missions, and church partnerships.

In the past decade, a growing, and substantial, number of congregations came to no longer view missions as a program or agency to support. On the contrary, many churches view mission as a central part of their identity as the body of the Christ. Stated differently, the congregation does not simply support missionaries, but views itself as missionary (a missionary ecclesiology). A sharp increase in congregations entering into long term, global, partnerships reflect this change. This trend represents a paradigm shift for many congregations. The trend also represents a paradigm shift for mission agencies and long-term missionaries. Rather than simply sending multiple work groups, this form of partnership focuses on complex humanitarian issues. Some congregations view this new focus as a way for congregants to live their Christian faith, gaining credibility in areas where people tended to see the church as myopic and self-serving.

Anthropologist Robert Priest describes "evangelicals . . . engaging in holistic mission out of a deep conviction that such patterns of positive public Christian presence are essential for credible Christian witness."[2] According to Priest, the new movement in some congregations reflects:

> (N)ot solely a movement from spaces where there are Christians to spaces where there are not, but rather a movement from spaces where there are Christians and churches that have extensive material resources to other spaces where there are significant numbers of Christians and churches that live under circumstances of material poverty and social constraint.[3]

2. Priest, *A New Era of Mission is Upon Us*, 2011, 300

3 , Ibid., 297

These holistic, grass roots, approaches to global Christian efforts represent an important shift in missions.

Evangelical missions of the 20th Century, the time Schrieter calls "second wave," focused largely on evangelism and church planting to non-evangelized areas. Congregations accomplished evangelistic goals through the work of long term missionaries sent by mission agencies.

The current shift, seen in some congregational partnerships, builds on both the previous and the current work of long-term missionaries, many who establish churches and institutions. However one also finds a movement toward congregations networking with multiple organizations to address global humanitarian issues as another form of mission. This movement involves congregations that seek connections (many times beyond their own theological tradition) to help them negotiate networks with a variety of entities, including non-U.S. congregations. This shift, therefore presents potential for addressing global challenges such as HIV/AIDS, drought, hunger, and large scale disaster relief.

The rapid growth of this grass-roots phenomenon appears relatively recent. Using one of the most common terms to describe this movement, "partnership," raises a challenge. Partnership, as a term, can indicate very different things to different people. For a westerner, the term can indicate business transactions with a focus on task completion. Non-westerners may think of the concept, "partnership" in relational terms. They might use friendship terminology as a means to meeting needs. For these reasons, the term partnership needs to be appropriately contextualized and applied in each location. I have chosen to use the term "congregational mission partnerships" to describe the current phenomenon since this pattern initiated from local congregations, rather than missiologists or mission agencies. Congregational mission also expresses the missional concept of the congregation as missionary.

Some people view partnerships as toxic, as a return to colonialist missions that appear donor dependent and one directional. Others doubt it possible to maintain a balanced relationship between Christians with an overabundance of financial resources and Christians desperately needing those same resources. The majority of participants in my research, however, find renewal within their congregation through these partnerships. Pastors are also discovering new ways to lead their congregations in mission. These congregations, while not accustomed to intense cross-cultural ministry, desire encouragement and direction to help them form healthy patterns for long term global ministry. Congregations in partnerships deliberate how they can engage in mission across cultures in meaningful ways. Beyond their deliberation, they question how these partnerships can foster renewal in their congregations that results in a mission vision for their neighboring community, work, and personal lives.

THE GOAL OF THIS BOOK

This book does not provide a prescription for a new mission program. Neither does it offer a design for partnerships developed in a mission headquarters or seminary. Although I have translated research findings through missiological and theological lenses, this book provides a description of a new, grass roots, movement; one begun in local congregations. More specifically this book designates common patterns for healthy global partnerships observed in these congregational partnerships. I do not hold up any of the congregations as a perfect model. Neither would the people in these congregations suggest that they have all of the answers.

However, as these congregations make mistakes, they learn some approaches prove more effective than others. Common patterns emerge for best practices in partnerships. I found these patterns in large as well as small congregations, in a variety of partnership relationships, and in a variety of global contexts. These patterns provide a compass, rather than a roadmap, for congregations journeying into mission with partners around the world.

The specific structure of the partnership in a mega-church, with an abundance of medical professionals working to address HIV/AIDs, proves very different than the partnership structure involving a congregation of 150 people, or one of 500 people, coming alongside those in Kenya to install water wells. The structure also looks different when inviting a congregation of 1000 people to come alongside church planters in Asia. I, therefore, do not attempt to provide a step-by-step guide for all partnerships. This book does offer common patterns found in all of these varied structures of healthy partnerships. Congregations can build upon the suggested healthy patterns. So churches develop appropriate structures and strategies both consistent with their congregation and with their ministry partner's context. Beyond this goal, these patterns serve as a guide to designing healthy mission relationships that will free the global church to live into its identity as the body of Christ.

TYPES OF PARTNERSHIPS

As a point of clarification related to the use of the term partnership, many ministries describe themselves as partnerships. One approach, commonly called partnership, more accurately describes a sponsorship since one finds little reciprocity in finances, ideas, or planning. More specifically, the extent to which there is shared governance defines sponsorships. These partnerships include ministries such as The Jesus Film Partnership, disaster relief partnerships, child sponsorship partnerships, and other ministries that move strategies and finances primarily from western, industrialized, nations to majority world locations. This approach to partnership often involves individuals, or clusters of individuals, within the congregation. Normally these sponsorships actually rely on a partnership between the donors and a mission agency.

Short-term missions describe a second form of partnership. The phenomenon of short-term mission remains widespread in U.S. churches and universities. Not too long ago, the youth pastor's job description might implicitly include summer camp trips. Congregants now expect youth pastors to lead students on either urban, or international, short-term mission trips. Increasingly, Christian universities require or encourage all students to participate in short-term mission trips during summer, fall, or spring breaks. In many congregations, groups of middle age to older adults participate in construction teams. A growing number of medical professionals include short-term medical mission in their resume, complete with pictures of their mission involvement alongside their diplomas on office walls.

Ministries often attach the word "partnership" to short-term mission when short-term mission teams continue to go to one location for more than just one trip. Serial short-term missions may provide a better description of such relationships. Many people who regularly lead short-term missions find that repeating their short-term mission trip to the same place proves more effective than setting up new locations for every time they have a trip. These serial trips build relationships with people on site, as well as with the missionaries or facilitators working with them. Like sponsorships, individuals in a congregation, or university, normally lead the trip. Trips include a select group of participants, rather than whole congregations.

A third form of partnership, called congregational partnership, serves as the focus of this book. Readers will find some commonalities between congregational partnerships and the other two approaches mentioned. Readers will also find unique aspects of congregational mission that present great potential, as well as great challenge. More specifically, congregational partnerships tend to be driven by the congregation's lead-pastor rather than rely on lay leadership, or a mission agency for motivation and guidance. Congregational partnerships involve the whole congregation in mission. Furthermore, congregational partnerships often (although not always) address large humanitarian issues beyond the scope of the previous two approaches to sponsorship/partnership. To provide a broad definition, congregational partnership involves two or more congregations, or groups of congregations that differ in resources, culture, and typically nationality, yet work together toward a common mission.

HEALTHY PATTERNS OF CONGREGATIONAL PARTNERSHIPS

Five patterns of healthy congregational partnerships form the framework of this book. These patterns emerge from research derived in congregations heavily involved in congregational partnerships. The congregations vary from mega churches of 7,000 congregants, to small churches of fifty members. The congregations surveyed represent a variety of theological traditions. Furthermore, the congregations maintain different approaches to partnership. Other than their Christian faith, the common strand among these congregations entails a commitment to a long-term relationship with another congregation, or area, beyond their own nationality. This commitment is based on a common mission.

None of the congregations studied gave a perfect example of a healthy congregational partnership. Each church encountered learning edges. In addition, each of them possessed strengths to add to the understanding of best practices.

Although this writing includes a deliberate arrangement of the five patterns, readers should not assume a sequential order. The patterns do not build on one another. Chapter five, for example, uses missional theology in conceptualizing congregational mission as a missionary ecclesiology (the church as missionary). This chapter also describes the practical challenge congregations face as they balance between foreign missions and local missions. Some readers might assume that the theological framework should be the first chapter to serve as a guide for mission involvement. The author's perspective remains that mission and theology prove inseparable. Whether one begins with context, mission practice, or theology, proves to be a moot issue. However, given the nucleus of this book surfaces through ethnographic studies, the chapters begin with the way congregations self-describe their partnership. None of the congregations in this study define their partnership in theological terms. They did, however, describe practical issues one can effectively address through ecclesiological and missiological frameworks.

The first four chapters directly relate to the complexities of cross-cultural partnerships discovered in surveys and interviews with congregations and their partners. Culture provides a major challenge in these types of partnerships. Issues of power, trust, and reciprocity, coupled with financial inequity, prove equally challenging. The first four chapters address these challenges as partners work toward a common mission, reciprocal relationships, and good communication. Note all of these are patterns would benefit transnational Non-Governmental Organizations (NGOs) and other non-Christian specific organizations. Chapter five moves these patterns beyond tools for effective cross-cultural negotiation. The chapter stresses the redemptive nature of reciprocal relationships, both with people in distant countries, and with others in a local setting. In broader terms, congregants can see loving relationships as the DNA of the Christian faith.

Chapter six describes the organizational framework that allows for collective impact as congregations address global issues such as HIV/AIDS, drought, human trafficking, and gender-based violence. This chapter describes the emerging catalytic role that congregations possess when strategically aligned in collective impact. The patterns include:

1. *A Common Agenda.* The first pattern of healthy partnerships acknowledges various participants in the partnership possess a common agenda. This agenda provides a shared vision for change, with a common understanding of the problem, and a joint approach to solving it through agreed upon actions.

2. *Reciprocity.* A second pattern of healthy partnerships includes mutually reinforcing activities (reciprocity). Ideal partnerships allow each partner to teach as well as learn from one another. This pattern demands that partners intentionally strive to avoid paternalism and dependency. It also implies that relationships remain as important as ministry projects.

3. *Clear Communication.* A third common pattern of healthy partnerships involves intentional effort toward clear, quality, communication in the partnership. This pattern demands

consistent, open, communication that builds trust. The pattern implies a need for cultural brokers who can navigate communication. More than any other factor, the role of a cultural broker provides the most essential factor for healthy and effective congregational partnerships. The cultural broker's ability to bridge between the various parts of a partnership determines its success or failure.

4. *God's mission.* Fourth, healthy partnerships focus on God's mission. This emphasis implies an explicit connection to the larger vision of mission. The vision connects partnership activities to local mission involvement. This emphasis also implies intentional effort to help participants integrate their mission experience with their work and life.

5. *Platform organization.* Fifth, healthy Partnerships often work with a platform organization for coordination. Congregations with partnerships address complex global issues by connecting to a larger platform organization. Those congregations thrive, possessing potential for a long-term impact.

A SNAP SHOT OF THE CONGREGATIONAL PARTNERSHIPS

The five patterns of healthy partnerships originally emerged from in-depth research of the partnership between a Nazarene congregation in Bethany, Oklahoma and a variety of church associations, medical institutions, and governmental, non-governmental organizations in Swaziland. The Swaziland Partnership proved complex. It involved a large U.S. congregation and an historic mission field in Swaziland, yet also a country suffering from the effects of HIV/ AIDS. In all, I conducted 200 ethnographic interviews between both locations. People in Swaziland gave great insight into healthy approaches for U.S. churches to partner with African churches. Swazis also revealed some of the challenges of working with a partner that has enormous resources. Conversely the U.S. congregants described the impact Swazis had on their congregation and upon themselves personally. Research interviews also included a focus group of African leaders from the countries of Botswana, Lesotho, Namibia, South Africa and Swaziland. Exploring the long-term impact of these types of partnerships, I conducted additional interviews with older missionaries and leaders who were present during an earlier era of mission history in Swaziland.

The research on this relationship provided a great resource for understanding this particular type of congregational partnership. This partnership, however, involved a sizable congregation with substantial resources. So, one might question if the principles discovered in this research would also apply to smaller congregations. Would they also apply to different types of partnerships or to larger congregations? The next step involved surveying a variety of congregations that fit the general description of a congregational partnership. The goal entailed seeing if the patterns found in the original research applied to a congregation of 150, or a congregation of 7,000. Beyond the difference of congregational size, I conducted research to see if these patterns proved consistent in differing global contexts. However, readers should remember the primary research for this writing was the Swaziland/Bethany First Partnership. In some cases I had brief meetings to understand one aspect of their partnership better, such as the role of cultural broker or mission pastor; in other cases I collected data and had formal interviews. The following overview provides a snap shot of the partnerships surveyed for this study:

Swaziland/Bethany First Church of the Nazarene (BFC).

BFC is a congregation of 2500 people with a ten year partnership to address HIV/AIDS in the most infected country of the world: Swaziland. An historic Nazarene congregation, BFC has traditionally supported a denominational mission structure with annual offerings of $300,000 to $400,000 a year. In 2007, BFC decided to begin a large-scale partnership with Swaziland, the oldest mission field in the Church of the Nazarene, to address the HIV/AIDS epidemic in that country. Over the next three years this church sent more than 400 volunteers from their congregation. Beyond increased volunteerism and increased mission giving, the partnership appears unique in the synergy produced by a network of relationships that produced catalytic results. One grant writer works in a brokering role for the Bethany congregation, helping to secure private and federal funds. He states,

> BFC in time, donated medical equipment (shipped containers) and, actual contributions have generated about five million dollars in resources. These five million dollars has allowed us to access, between Coca-Cola, the CDC and USAID about $6.5 million in actual grants or contracts.[4]

More recently, members of BFC initiated a solar panel water well project within the Swaziland Partnership. The concept received recognition through the Energy Global World Award in 2012. This award resulted in Coca-Cola Africa Foundation grants of $30 million. The concept also generated $23 million in matching funds from USAID for further development of similar water systems throughout the continent of Africa. Although the grants indirectly related to the Swaziland Partnership, this type of partnership represented an emerging paradigm. Large congregations, with networking structures, may partner directly with multiple organizations. The partnership generated a greater impact in a specific area of the world, as well as within the congregation.

Harvest Ministries/Jacob's Well

One could describe Jacob's Well, a church in Kansas City, Missouri, as a missional, non-denominational congregation. The 500-member congregation engages in a partnership with City Harvest Ministries in Nairobi, Kenya. Jacob's Well and City Harvest minister with the people of Asilong village in Pokot, the northwestern part of Kenya. This relationship, started in 2007, bloomed into a sustainable, long-term project. Creative relationships between Jacob's Well and City Harvest Ministries opened the door for the two congregations to

---

4. James Copple 2010, e-mail message to author

work together in ministry at the third location. More than eleven water wells have been installed through this partnership.

Vida Abundante/Boston Hingham Church

The Hingham church includes a congregation of approximately fifty people maintaining a partnership with *Vida Abundante* Church in Guatemala City, Guatemala. This community provides an example of a non-resource dependent partnership. These churches found creative ways to build relationships, celebrating events in the lives of the two congregations by communicating in their different languages through social media.

Zambia/Oklahoma City (OKC) First Church

OKC First, a denominational congregation of about 1000 people, continues a ten-year strategic partnership with Zambia in community development. This partnership includes a long-term missionary in Zambia. The missionary helps OKC First and Zambian congregations build strategies that assist Zambian leaders while encouraging self-supporting practices in Zambian churches.

Cuba/Lenexa Central Church.

Central Church in Lenexa Kansas finds itself in the beginning stages of a partnership with a group of churches in Cuba. Many aspects of this partnership remain at an early stage. Still, I chose to explore this partnership since it represents collaboration with churches in a country where they cannot supply a missionary or representative from their church. Mature, historic, Cuban congregations partner with Central Church primarily as a way to construct new churches and school buildings.

Heal the Kids(Nairobi)/Vancouver First Church of the Nazarene

This church of approximately 150 people maintains a partnership in Nairobi, Kenya. The partnership is with an organization called "Heal the Kids," a group that organizes schools in the slums of Kenya. This year the Vancouver church raised 25,000 dollars to build classrooms for a schoolhouse.

Beyond these congregations I cultivated specific conversations with many other leaders about aspects of their partnerships. I have talked with mission pastors and pastors at Willow Creek, Church of the Resurrection UMC, and Olathe College Church of the Nazarene. I also met with a group of about forty-five mission directors serving as staff in United Methodist Churches running 1,000 or more in average attendance.

Collectively, these interviews and conversations provide a research background for the five patterns of mission practice that outline the rest of the text. As readers navigate the remaining chapters, remember that the patterns reflect the actions and attitudes of a number of people, all joined together in their "common mission" for the sake of the Kingdom of God.

2

A Shared Mission

If you want to go fast, go alone. If you want to go far, go together. (African Proverb)

Through him, we all have access to the Father by one Spirit. Consequently, (we) are no longer foreigners and aliens, but fellow citizens with God's people and members of God's household. (Ephesians 2:19)

THE FIRST PATTERN OF healthy partnerships acknowledges various participants in the partnership possessing a common agenda. This agenda provides a shared vision for change, with a common understanding of the problem, and a joint approach to solving it through agreed upon actions.

PROMISE AND RISK IN PARTNERSHIP

Whether marriage or ministry relationships, making commitments to long-term relationships provide a mixture of risk and fulfillment. With such a high, long term risk, partners should enter into these type of relationships with great care and with the direction of those who can give counsel. A congregation that dedicates resources and ministry in a global partnership makes a substantial commitment that includes risk, as well as potential success. Congregations located in areas often referred to as "host" locations, enter partnerships in a similar fashion. In doing so, they risk harmful patterns similar to colonialistic missions from the West. These patterns often overlooked the significance of the host location. Conversely, these churches also face the positive potential of ministry that would otherwise lie beyond their reach. Challenges within cross-cultural partnerships exist for both partners. Still, growing numbers of congregations decide to enter into partnerships with the hope of effective and meaningful ministry for both the local church and their partner in mission.

TWO MINISTRIES, TWO RESULTS

In the fall of 2007, I witnessed the beginning of such a partnership; one that would become the focus of my doctoral dissertation research. My wife and I traveled to the college town of Bethany Oklahoma where our daughter had just begun her first year of college. On Sunday morning, before returning home, the three of us attended a worship service at Bethany First Church of the Nazarene (BFC). Bethany First Church is a historic congregation established in 1909 and resides adjacent to a denominationally supported private university. With over 2000 people we attended the second worship service that Sunday morning.

A large pipe organ covered the front of the sanctuary, and massive stained glass windows accented the cathedral-like sanctuary. Everything about the service that morning seemed carefully orchestrated and predictable. The sermon, however, provided a turning point in the life of BFC. The turning point would motivate more than 400 people into personal mission involvement within three years. The pastor called the challenge a move toward "a new paradigm in mission."[1] That Sunday morning the pastor stated:

> HIV and AIDS now defines the greatest humanitarian crisis in the history of the world. Already 25 million people have died of this disease. Currently, 40 million people live with HIV and AIDS. 28 million live with the disease in Sub Saharan Africa and those are just the documented cases which may be a percentage of the real cases. Last year more than 3 million people died of AIDS. That is 8,000 people per day . . . AIDS has already killed more people than all the plagues, all the famines, all the natural disasters, all the wars in our entire history.

The pastor paused and then emphasized, "The AIDS epidemic is the greatest crisis of our day, but it is also the greatest opportunity for the church to be the church in a world that thinks the church will not show up." In an interview four years later, the pastor said this opportunity marked a high risk for the congregation. However, the decision also defined one of the most anointed moments of his ministry. The effort resulted in millions of dollars, invested through multiple organizations, extending the ministry of Christians in Swaziland caring for those suffering and dying from AIDS.

That morning, along with the congregation, I felt challenged by what I heard. At the same time, I was skeptical that one congregation, no matter how large, could effectively address something as big as the HIV/AIDS crisis in the most impacted country in the world.

More than a few NGO's and church groups attempted lesser goals with little or no success. Similarly, other Christian efforts addressed comparable challenges yet suffered very public, large-scale failure. In 2005, the Wall Street Journal publicized an example of these failures through an article about Bruce Wilkinson, the famous author of *The Prayer of Jabez*. Wilkinson possessed a vision similar to that of Bethany First Church. Wilkinson moved much of his earnings to address the HIV/AIDS crisis in the country of Swaziland

---

1. David Busic, sermon *"HIV/AIDS: An African Crisis & Our Response"* October 2007

and encouraged others to give to his vision. The following reference to Wilkinson's efforts appeared in the Wall Street Journal article:

> Mr. Wilkinson won church loads of followers in Swaziland, but left them bereft and confused. He gained access to top Swazi officials but alienated them with his demands. And his departure left critics convinced he was just another in a long parade of outsiders who had come to Africa making big promises and quit the continent when local people didn't bend to their will.[2]
>
> Wilkinson, according to the article, abandoned his attempts after failing to untangle the cultural nuances of the monarchy.[3]

Many of Wilkinson's strategies and objectives for Swaziland seemed similar to those of Bethany First Church. Similar to BFC, Wilkinson seemed struck by the plight of orphaned children in Swaziland and felt compelled to action. As with BFC, Wilkinson arranged a large conference where Swazi pastors openly discussed AIDS. Similar to Wilkinson, BFC dreamed big dreams, made sacrifices in the process, and followed what they thought reflected God's leading. Unlike Wilkinson, BFC had a degree of success where Wilkinson struggled. BFC efforts led to expanded partnerships and praise from the Swazi government.

As we look at these two approaches to the same challenge, an important question remains. What is the difference between this local church initiative and Wilkinson's attempts alongside others having limited or no success?" In broader terms, "what can we learn from these two partnerships that can lead us to healthy congregational partnerships?"

In 2011-2012, I began research of the fourth year of the Swaziland Partnership. I found the partnership between Bethany First Church and Swaziland, similar to Wilkinson's efforts, included cultural challenges and suffered occasional mistakes. The BFC/Swaziland partnership, however, proved most effective when

2. Phillips, "Unanswered Prayers."
3. Phillips, "Unanswered Prayers."

intentional efforts focused on a shared vision and a common approach to ministry.

Adopting a common mission proves difficult for congregations, or individuals, from cultures like those in the U.S., cultures that seem predominantly individualist in nature. The United States, as well as many countries in Africa, includes individuals with a variety of cultural preferences. Still cultural preferences in African countries remain predominantly collectivist, while cultural preferences in the U.S. prove predominantly individualist. A sense of self-reliance and independence provide one marker of individualist cultures. U.S. culture accentuates individual success or failure. In contrast, collectivist cultures, such as those found in much of Africa, recognize one's identity resides largely as a function of one's membership and role in a group (e.g., the family, the work team). In collectivist cultures, the survival and success of the group ensure the well-being of the individual. The model of living and working in community proves familiar for those who live in predominantly collectivist cultures such as Swaziland.

Although variations in cultural preferences appear within any society, general cultural tendencies played a major role in efforts like Bruce Wilkinson, as well as those of Bethany First Church. Both actors tended to default to western business models of individualism and communication. The difference between failure and success in both circumstances rested with an openness to allow for African models of decision making, communication and planning.

LESSONS ABOUT COMMON MISSION
FROM AFRICA

Many countries in Africa suffer from a devastating history of colonialism and dependency. Ironically, people in these areas also possess a rich cultural understanding of relationships and healthy partnerships. The relational concepts learned from Africa prove helpful as congregations build strong interactions that avoid destructive dependency or paternalism.

In spite of great challenges, Africa can teach the rest of the world how to live in an interconnected community. Ubuntu defines a concept in South Africa and many other African countries, describing collectivist culture. Barbara Nussbaum defines *Ubuntu* as "the spirit which shapes the art of being human together."[4] The concept may seem challenging for those from individualistic cultures. However, Ubuntu rests on the notion that our primary identity emerges from the identity that we have together. Nussbaum states, "In essence, *Ubuntu*, a *Nguni* word from South Africa, addresses our interconnectedness, our common humanity, and the responsibility to each other that flows from our connection."[5] This concept possesses great implications for the Christian church facing a global environment of greed and political divisions; as well as global challenges of poverty, drought, human trafficking and injustice. Furthermore, our common Christian identity offers renewal for the global church, shaping all other identities.

I encountered examples of Ubuntu while doing research in Swaziland. Early in my time, I spent a day visiting several of the sites where the partnership between one U.S. church and Swaziland churches installed water pumps. At one of the sites, I visited a church in a rural community called *Ntondozi*. As I met with the pastor, she described how countless people in their community died of AIDS related illnesses, leaving behind young children. She talked about the people of her church that were caring for many of these children. The people of this rural church cared for the orphaned children by dividing the food from their own homes and giving some of their own children's clothes. These women described how their church coordinated with their community, providing a location at their church for children to receive both a meal and elementary education.

While at this church, I interviewed three women leaders in the congregation. We sat on wooden benches underneath a large shade tree. I asked them about the water well which their new church partner from the U.S just the day before had helped

4. Nancy Nussbaum, "Ubuntu," 21.

5. Ibid.

install. I noticed that there was a fence around the church property to protect the orphaned children that the church cared for during the day. Various water outlets serviced the church. One could find four to five outlets throughout the property: for the garden areas, the rest room, cooking area, as well as one outlet just outside the property. I asked the women, "Why did you put water access on the outside of the fence where everyone from the community can freely take water instead of putting the outlet on the inside where the church could control how much was being used?" The three women laughed as though this was an odd question. They responded, "We put the water outlet outside of the fence because we are Christian. We didn't make the water; God did. If we kept it to ourselves, we would not be Christian. We have to share with those around us."

The Ntondozi women's connection of their Christian identity with the water wells provides an important distinction, even within a collectivist society. A couple of days before visiting Ntondozi, I interviewed some community leaders in a different part of Swaziland. Their village possessed a water well, one installed beside a school but not operated by a church. The leaders indicated their water system provided for the school and a medical clinic. I asked the school if this water well benefited the community near the school. Although the well contained sufficient water for the whole community, leaders feared providing community access would deplete the water. In this instance, a scarcity mentality overrode both collectivist and Christian possibilities.

However, Ubuntu couples Christian identity with community, providing a foundation for a common mission. As congregations work together, they discover the crucial understanding that God's mission is not ours to hoard. One must also learn how to engage effectively with partners who share a mutual Christian identity, even if not a cultural identity.

A shared mission between congregations of differing cultures resembles a dance in which one partner will lead at different times. This metaphor implies a common understanding of the roles of each partner in order to avoid disjointed movements. A story told by missiologist Miriam Adeney illustrates how the African perspective views this disjointed dance in missions. An African leader approached Adeney saying, "Let me tell you a story."

> Elephant and Mouse were best friends. One day Elephant said, "Mouse, let's have a party!" Animals gathered from far and near. They ate; they drank. They sang and danced. Nobody celebrated more and danced harder than Elephant. After the party was over, Elephant exclaimed, "Mouse, did you ever go to a better party? What a blast!"
>
> But Mouse did not answer.
>
> "Mouse where are you?" Elephant called. He looked around for his friend, and then shrank back in horror. There, at Elephant's feet, lay Mouse. His little body was ground into the dirt, smashed by the big feet of his exuberant friend, Elephant.
>
> "Sometimes that is what it is like to do mission with you Americans," the African storyteller commented. "It is like dancing with an Elephant."[6]

Partnerships between different cultures can feel exhilarating. Joint ministry efforts can bear results beyond what any congregation could do alone. However, defining roles within the partnership makes a difference between destructive or healthy interactions.

The example of Wilkinson's efforts proves very similar to the elephant and mouse story. Wilkinson, like many well-meaning North Americans, had good intentions to use their resources to benefit others. In the process, however, dancing with those of other cultures becomes more complex than imagined.

HISTORICAL MISSION FIELDS AND PARTNERSHIPS

Bethany First Church possessed a major advantage with the historic partnership their denomination already maintained with Swaziland. Many denominations have a pioneer area that symbolizes missions for them. Within the Church of the Nazarene,

6. Adeney, *Daughters of Islam*, 189.

Swaziland represents this area, thanks to the Schmelzenbach family who pioneered the mission work beginning in 1905. The story includes hardships and dangers as the missionary family lost children to disease. The Schmelzenbach stories, describing how the gospel slowly took root, became well known throughout the denomination by 1928. Since the Schmelzenbachs went to Africa, such stories became folklore, recounted in churches both in the U.S. and in Swaziland.

By 1928, the Schmelzenbach stories coupled with newer stories of medical missionary David Hynd from Scotland, creating greater support for the mission work. The denomination began to send an increasing number of missionaries to Swaziland. Schmelzenbach's and Hynd's emphasis on mission with a threefold focus through medicine, education, and evangelization established a pattern of building churches alongside medical clinics and schools. The Fitkin family's large donation to build a hospital in memory of their son provided one poignant example as that donation culminated in the construction of Raleigh Fitkin Memorial Hospital.

This pattern continues to characterize Nazarene missions in Swaziland, integrating evangelism, education and medicine. The same Nazarene infrastructure provides a framework of schools, clinics and churches throughout the country, one that served a healthy Bethany First Church partnership to address HIV/AIDS. In contrast to Wilkinson's efforts to fashion an infrastructure in Swaziland, BFC and Nazarenes build on the denomination's historical foundations, including good relationships with the monarchy.

However, the work in Swaziland also appeared similar to other mission agencies and evangelical denominations undergoing change. By the 1970's and 1980's the church growth movement gained momentum. At the same time, the Church of the Nazarene transitioned away from institutionalized mission through medicine and education. The focus moved toward evangelism and church development. The move indicated a polemic shift for those in Swaziland, particularly with redirecting the missionaries away from medical care. Although the strategic move did result in the numeric growth of churches throughout Africa, Swaziland struggled with dependency. Swazis found it difficult maintaining a structure for medical care previously supported by funding from outside of Swaziland.

In 1986, about the same time that the Church of the Nazarene decided to refocus mission funds, Swaziland reported it's first case of HIV/AIDs. Since 1986, the disease spread rapidly. The Human Development Index of the UN provided one consequence of the pervasive growth rate of HIV/AIDS in Swaziland. Life expectancy fell from sixty-one years in 2000 to thirty-two years in 2009. The United Nations Development Program reported that if the country's epidemic continued unabated, the "long term existence of Swaziland as a country will be seriously threatened."

A pastor in Swaziland stated, "in Swaziland everyone is either infected by AIDs or affected by AIDS." In such an environment, it is common for Swaziland pastors to care for orphaned children whose parents have died of AIDS. As noted earlier, many (possibly all) of the congregations in Swaziland pooled congregational resources to care for the growing number of orphaned children. Glori Dlamini, a pastor in Ntondozi, recounted that there were many children in the community near her church who had lost one or both parents to AIDS. Dlamini said it was common for extended family and friends to add these children to their family, providing for the children out of their limited resources. Since the number of orphaned children remains so high, and because many of these families deal with illnesses related to AIDS, Rev. Dlamini noted people in her church began to share clothes that were for their own children. Beyond clothing, they also shared food from their kitchens in order to help these families and the children. Many of the people of the church and nearly all pastors bring these children to live in their homes as well. The impact of AIDS on Swaziland, coupled with a difficult mission transition in a region dependent on medical missionaries and financial support, posed a formidable challenge for Swazis.

In spite of the losses in health care, people in churches of Swaziland described how they were grateful for their discipleship, establishing a Christian foundation received from the missionaries.

They described the sacrifice Christian missionaries made bringing the gospel to Swaziland with great emotion and respect. They also described their love and friendships with missionaries. However, they also voiced concerns about the dependence the missionaries had built, and the lack of Swazi preparation for the missionaries' sudden departure.

Bethany First Church began a dialog with Swazi leaders about a partnership, but with diverse motivations. BFC representatives viewed the partnership primarily as a way to come alongside Swazis by addressing HIV/AIDS. Swaziland participants viewed the partnership in a similar manner. However, they also saw the partnership as a way to heal the pain of separation from their partners in the U.S. The U.S. congregation saw their partnership as a type of business transaction, while those in Swaziland viewed the partnership as Ubuntu and collective Christian identity.

Partnerships with historic mission areas such as Swaziland represent the potential to build on foundations that make partnerships more effective. They also pose the possibility of working alongside mature Christians in the host location that can share leadership. In some cases, these types of partnerships may also bring healing from hurtful transitions of the past. Partnerships may present a means of renewal in areas that churches are waning in vibrancy, either in the host country or the guest country. Partnerships with historic mission areas represent renewal and potential for healthy relations. However, practitioners need to take great caution addressing colonialist patterns of the past. Partners must avoid dependency throughout the planning and implementation process.

Healthy partnerships (the first pattern) inform these types of practices. These partnerships include a common agenda, a shared vision for change, with a common understanding of the problem. The partnership also shared a joint approach to solving problems through agreed upon actions. The partnerships also reflect emerging trends in other areas of business and social science known as "collective impact."

COLLECTIVE IMPACT AND PARTNERSHIPS

A cutting edge approach to address large-scale social issues in the U.S. draws on similar principles as Ubuntu. Collective Impact addresses the coordination needed within strategic partnerships responding to large-scale social issues. One finds the concept in current business literature such as the *Stanford Review, New York Times, and Harvard Buisness Review.* Readers will find a detailed description to Collective Impact in chapter six. The concept's intersection with an understanding of Ubuntu warrants its current consideration. Collective Impact addresses the dilemma that "large-scale social change requires broad cross-sector coordination, instead of intervention of individual organizations."[7] In a column for the New York Times David Berstein describes collective impact as follows:

> The idea is to create a network that links numerous organizations—including those in government, civil society and the business sector. In addition, Collective Impact assists networks in aligning systematically, and coordinating efforts around a clearly defined goal, like improving education, combating childhood obesity, or cleaning rivers. It may strike some readers as obvious, but it represents a departure from "business as usual." In addition, the concept strikes me as one of the most important experiments occurring in the social sector today.[8]

Similar to Ubuntu, Kania and Kramer argue collective impact theory offers strategic and collective work among multiple organizations. The strategy proves more effective than the aggregate sum of organizations working individually.

Many organizations and individuals face frustrations and failure, or experience limited impact in relation to investment, when addressing something as large scale as the HIV/AIDS epidemic in the most affected country in the world. These theories

---

7. Kania, "Collective Impact," 36.

8. Ibid.

present a challenge to traditional mission approaches. Conversely, the theories offer great potential for the church playing a key role addressing global challenges.

UBUNTU AND SOCIAL THEORY

The concept of Ubuntu also intersects with a number of social capital theories within American and missiological circles. In very broad terms, social capital represents the benefits occurring to individuals or groups because of their interaction. An example of this might be the social ties that one has with their neighbors. Relationships are developed that result in neighbors helping one another and looking out for one another. Social capital theory, applied to congregational partnerships, helps clarify the social benefits within groups of individuals who travel together for multiple mission trips. The social capital relationships and networks formed in a Collective Impact arrangement demonstrate how these connections are augmented when multiple groups strategically work together. The outcome of these strategic partnerships is substantially greater than what a single mission agency, denomination, or an NGO (non-government agency) alone can generate.

Social theorists and missiologists often describe these relationships using various key terms like "bonding," "bridging," or "linking" social capital. Ultimately the impact on communities proves greater than the sum of all of the varying efforts when agencies act alone.

Bonding Social Capital

Perhaps "bonding social capital" defines the most evident aspect of social capital in congregational mission partnerships. Bonding social capital occurs among close, resilient, connections within a group, such as a short-term mission team or congregation. Researchers, such as Robert Wuthnow and Robert Priest, document the bonding that happens within the group of people who travel together. This bonding provides one of the greatest impacts of short-term missions, and congregational partnerships. More recent research discovered a link between bonding in a local congregation and participation in volunteer activities such as mission trips. Leading American sociologists, Robert Putnam, Robert Wuthnow and Nancy Ammerman provide different interpretations of the correlation between networks formed in congregations and volunteering for activities such as mission trips. Yet, a consistent strand links Putnam's, Wuthnow's, and Ammerman's conclusions. They imply a correlation between the religious networking relationships within congregations and global networking that moves congregations toward partnerships and transnational collaboration.

In his book, *American Grace*, Robert Putnam presents a "twist" to bonding social capital theory. The twist specifically emerges as congregations act to create religious, social networks. According to Putnam, congregations that form bonding social capital within the church often engage in volunteering, or what Putnam classifies as "good deeds." Additional congregational studies literature, like Nancy Ammerman's *Pillars of Faith* and sociologist Robert Wuthnow's 2009 book, *Boundless Faith,* connect the dynamic of congregations with social bonding or religious networking. A fascinating aspect of Putnam's theory emerges when considering the number of non-Christian people who become involved in congregational partnerships. A reality that seems similar to Christian participants volunteering for projects while not identified as members of the partnership congregation. In many of the partnerships, numerous individuals came from other faith traditions, or did not share the Christian beliefs of the congregation. The Swaziland partnership included non-Christian medical professionals who resonated with the church's mission to address HIV/AIDS. Some of those outside of church membership appeared the most active in the partnership.

Sociologist, Robert Wuthnow also points to the importance of religious networking for the local congregation. Unlike Putnam, Wuthnow makes the point that there is a direct connection between faith and mission engagement. Furthermore, Wutnow argues that this type of volunteering indicates religious vitality in the United States. Nancy Ammerman makes a similar argument. Her extensive congregational study, conducted between 1997 and 2003, documents the direct connection between faith and service as the communities of faith. Ammerman discovered participants who defined themselves as: "under obligation to 'serve the world' in addition to serving their own members."[9] Unlike Putman, Ammerman observes other religions did not display the same emphasis on serving others, spreading the faith, and volunteerism, prevalent in Christian congregations. This insight indicates there might be a correlation between faith and volunteerism. This factor may be less dependent on a particular theological tradition than on a connection with the essence of being Christian.

Bridging Social Capital

Similar to the concept of Ubuntu, social capital theory maintains a core understanding that relationships remain vitally important. Stated differently, the social networks, formed in relationships, provide a valuable asset. Interaction between people with differing resources enables people to build a greater sense of global belonging. Furthermore the interaction allows opportunity to address issues previously thought impossible. This engagement brings benefits for all involved.

Robert Priest describes the critical and explicit connection between the concept of social capital and short-term mission.[10] Studying short-term mission teams in Peru, Priest notes: "when Peruvian *evangelicos* join collaboratively with gringos from abroad, they often find that schools, English language schools, University classrooms, jails, and hospitals which normally limit access to *evangelicos* open their doors wide."[11] This form of social capital known as bridging social capital occurs when Christians from limited financial resource areas productively partner with

9. Ammerman, *Pillars of Faith*, 115.

10. Priest,"*Peruvian Churches Acquire Linking Social Capital Through Short-Term Mission Partnerships,*" 175.

11. Ibid, 184.

resource rich Christians from other world settings. Quality relationships remain crucial in effective long-term congregational mission. The relationships, however, reflect more than mere social relationships and networks.

PRACTICAL IMPLICATIONS FOR CONGREGATIONAL PARTNERSHIPS

The first pattern of healthy congregational partnership offers a corrective to unhealthy colonialist mission practices, and one directional mission projects. This pattern emphasizes: 1) a common agenda, 2) a shared vision for change based on a common understanding of the problem and 3) a joint approach to solving problems through agreed upon actions.

This pattern highlights the dynamics of a common mission between partners with different resources and different needs. Furthermore, this pattern assumes that all partners have needs as well as capital to offer to the partnership. Arguably, this approach represents one of the most challenging patterns to develop within a congregational partnership. It is, however, one of the most essential patterns for long term, effective mission partnerships.

Healthy congregational partnerships work toward a common mission, avoiding relationships defined primarily in terms of donors and recipients. This approach assumes the partner with greater financial resources willingly allows the partner with lesser financial resources both voice and vote in the partnership's agenda and the strategy. Furthermore, the partner in the host location willingly permits the partner from the different culture participation beyond financial gifts. The following two strategies work toward these objectives.

First, partners should begin by spending sufficient time defining the nature of the partnership. The definition includes a plan for the life span of the partnership and a means for mutual accountability. This planning time proves vital. Most congregations included in this book's study invested considerable time together before the actual partnership began. Pastors and key leaders visited (some several times) the host location in order to listen and dialog with their potential partners. By listening, these visitors understood the need and develop a memorandum of understanding (MOU) with their partner. The MOU defines:

> a) A common understanding of the problem to be addressed. A vulnerability of U.S. congregations working in a new environment is the assumption that they understand the needs. Their assumptions develop as they view another culture through the lenses of their own culture. A vital initial step in any partnership involves defining real needs as understood and agreed upon by all partners. In the case of the Swaziland Partnership, from the beginning the Swazis, and those from the U.S, clearly defined the partnership as addressing HIV/AIDS in Swaziland.
>
> b) The second important aspect of the MOU includes a joint approach to mission activities through agreed upon actions. As the issues are clearly defined, the next step entails deciding the best approach to address the project. As both partners bring human and financial resources together, they collaboratively design their approach by carefully listening to one another.
>
> c) The third element of the MOU includes a common agenda. A frequent question surfaces in the research of congregations as their partners ask "who sets the agenda?" Who decides what projects deserve priority? Who makes decisions related to the use of funds? Who makes decisions for meals? Each question indicates the need for a common agenda.

I interviewed a focus group of African leaders from the countries of Botswana, Lesotho, Namibia, South Africa and Swaziland. I asked what it was like to have a partnership with North American churches. They were also asked about the greatest challenges in having a partnership with those churches. The number one response concerning greatest challenge of working in partnership with North Americans involved the issue of trust. Leaders stated that they felt North Americans did not trust Africans with food or money. Some expressed that, in some cases, Africans were invited to special shared meals with the North Americans. However, the Africans expressed they did not feel the meals they might offer Americans would be good enough. These perceptions possibly reflected a real lack of trust, or perhaps just the appearance of a lack of trust. Still, partners needed to define a common agenda, one related to food, money, duration of the projects, at the beginning of the partnership.

A second, vital, element of this first healthy pattern for congregational partnerships involves a willingness to listen and change plans. As in any relationship, partnerships must assume a great deal of flexibility and humility. The MOU established at the beginning of the partnership might better be seen as a compass instead of a road map. As partnerships develop, participants learn new insights. In many cases, these insights expose why some of the original intentions did not yield appropriate results. Many partnerships fall apart when they need to negotiate a new direction. The criteria for success did not include a critique whether or not partnership made changes to the original plans. Nearly all of the partnerships encountered changes in the process. The ability of partners to listen to one another and to make the necessary, mutually agreed upon, changes often determined the measure of success.

3

A Reciprocal Mission

If we see only differences, we will empower those who sow hatred rather than peace, and who promote conflict rather than cooperation. If we see only commonalities, we will either have to conform ourselves to others or they will have to conform to us; most likely, we will distort and dishonor both others and ourselves. Only when we see and respect both—undeniable differences that give communities a peculiar character and commonalities that bind them together—will we be able to honor each and promote the viable coexistence of all.

—MIRSOLAV VOLF, A PUBLIC FAITH[1]

A SECOND PATTERN OF healthy partnerships includes mutually reinforcing activities (reciprocity). Ideal partnerships allow each partner to teach as well as learn from one another. This pattern demands that partners intentionally strive to avoid paternalism and dependency. It also implies that relationships remain as important as ministry projects.

1. Volf, *A Public Faith* 2011, 140

MUTUALITY MATTERS

Reciprocity suggests that a partnership is not one directional. Reciprocity implies a mutual interchange that benefits both or all participants within a partnership. While vitally important, reciprocity also provides the most challenging aspect of congregational partnerships. Nearly all researched congregations agree that reciprocal relationships would greatly enhance their partnership. They struggle, however, developing a framework for these relationships, especially across linguistic barriers. Finances, or assistance flowing in one direction from one side of the partnership to the other, complicate these matters. Too often needy participants view the partner with the finances as an ATM machine or benevolent patron. On the other side, resource rich partners view the other partner, referred to as the host, as simply a recipient with nothing to add to the partnership. Within an environment of imbalanced resources, reciprocity challenges the most experienced cross-cultural minister, yet proves vital for a healthy partnership.

This chapter demonstrates the need, as well as the challenge, of reciprocity in partnerships. Challenges appear through misinterpreted good intentions, even around something as typical as food, as participants move from one culture to another. The missionary movement in congregations, engaging in the complex task of cross-cultural mission, presents a further challenge for healthy partnerships. Drawing from the biblical example of Jesus sending out the disciples, this chapter points to Jesus' intention for those sent out to give hospitality, but likewise to receive hospitality from those they serve. Reciprocity evident in the giving and receiving of hospitality, begins to break down the barriers of paternalism and dependency. Reciprocity emerges as partners build trust through the partaking of food and resources. Finally this chapter provides models of relationships, models helpful to understanding the degree of reciprocity needed for specific types of partnerships.

TABLE MANNERS

U.S. Congregations often invite a pastor or leader from the host location to speak in the partner church. The approach signals a good gesture that symbolizes a reciprocal partnership. However, additional steps need to be made to pass beyond these symbolic gestures and move toward a more robust relationship of reciprocity. For instance, listening to host partners can help North Americans by providing insights for healthy partnerships. Issues of trust and reciprocity often appear as important themes, frequently emerging when we listen to people in Africa, Latin America, and other world areas who host U.S. partners.

When I asked people in Africa what it was like to work in partnership with a U.S. or Canadian partner, the Africans normally expressed gratitude and love for those who came to them. Africans also expressed surprise that people continued to return to them. They stated how happy they were with the installation of the water wells, new roofs on churches, and many other things accomplished. The people expressed genuine gratitude. People needing something as foundational to life as water remain grateful that someone cares enough to provide for their family and their community. However as one spends time with these host partners who receive benevolent guests, challenges also emerge.

Participants recount issues of reciprocity, often related to trust, through the fundamental resources of food and money. Asked, "how do people in your country normally celebrate events such as installing a water well or putting on roofs?" Swazi leaders responded they normally kill an animal, cook, and eat together as a celebration of appreciation. When asked if they ever celebrated with their U.S. partners by inviting their guests to eat a personally prepared meal, some leaders responded the celebration happened only a couple of times with small groups. Nearly all responded, however, that normally the U.S. guest took initiative and invited Africans, deciding on the venue, and setting the agenda for the evening. One African leader told how he once invited a small U.S. leadership group to eat with him at a restaurant, one where he planned to pay for the dinner. He sadly said the U.S guests responded by announcing they had money from their church. The U.S. participants felt they could pay for the meal easier than the Africans.

During some occasions, like special conferences, leaders inadvertently separated the dining location for Africans from the U.S. participants. U.S. participants saw providing meals as an expression of hospitality and friendship. However, they expressed concern that North Americans might get sick from native foods. Africans did not always share the same interpretation. We asked Africans why they didn't invite their U.S. guests to their table. They said that they would like to one day. However, they didn't feel like their possessions and homes proved good enough for those from the U.S.

On another occasion, a group from the U.S. rented a conference room in the nicest area hotel. Other than the opening devotion, all of the speakers for the day remained part of the U.S. guest team. Workshop themes included time management, bivocational ministry, and the use of art in worship. Afterward, we asked pastors if they ever invited their U.S. guests to a time that Africans led the teaching. They responded they did not feel they possessed anything good enough to teach. The group from the U.S. had good intentions. They wanted to respect their African hosts by providing a nice meeting place. The Americans wanted to give the best that they could offer through teaching. Unintentionally, many Africans received the implicit message that Americans could not trust African teaching. Implicitly the U.S. group taught Africans their organizational skills seemed inferior, that they did not have anything to teach the North Americans. As their colonialist predecessors, U.S. participants intended to share the blessings experienced from their own context with the Africans. Good and loving intentions, however, can often lead to unintentional consequences. In both examples, the guest partner did a great job of giving hospitality, but found it more challenging to receive hospitality from their hosts.

The following traditional Tanzanian story, recounted by missiologist Duane Elmer, accentuates the danger of assumption in the midst of good intentions:

> A story is told about a monkey and a fish. It seems a typhoon had temporarily stranded a monkey on an island. In a secure, protected place and waiting for the raging waters to recede, he spotted a fish swimming against the current. It seemed obvious to the monkey that the fish was struggling and in need of assistance. Being of kind heart, the monkey resolved to help the fish.
>
> A tree precariously dangled over the very spot where the fish was struggling. At considerable risk to himself the monkey moved far out on a limb, reached down and snatched the fish from the "threatening" waters. Immediately scurrying back to the safety of his shelter, he carefully laid the fish on dry ground. For a few moments the fish showed excitement, but soon settled into a peaceful rest. Joy and satisfaction swelled inside the monkey. He had helped another creature and he had done it successfully.[2]

Proverbs 19:2 states that it is not good to have zeal without knowledge. A similar British proverb is "zeal without knowledge is a runaway horse." Zeal defines the earnestness and good intentions that remain essential to the church. However, the congregation's enthusiasm, coupled with inexperience in cross-cultural ministry, can result in an inability to listen and receive help from their host. This approach can prove harmful, completely reversing the good intentions of congregations desiring to help.

A MISSIONARY CHURCH

JESUS SENDS OUT THE TWELVE

²These are the names of the twelve apostles: first, Simon (who is called Peter) and his brother Andrew; James son of Zebedee, and his brother John; ³Philip and

---

2. Elmer, *Cross-Cultural Connections*, 14.

> *Bartholomew; Thomas and Matthew the tax collector;*
> *James son of Alphaeus, and Thaddaeus; ⁴ Simon the Zealot*
> *and Judas Iscariot, who betrayed him.*
>
> *⁵ These twelve Jesus sent out with the following in-*
> *structions: "Do not go among the Gentiles or enter any*
> *town of the Samaritans. ⁶ Go rather to the lost sheep of*
> *Israel. ⁷ As you go, proclaim this message: 'The kingdom*
> *of heaven has come near.' ⁸ Heal the sick, raise the dead,*
> *cleanse those who have leprosy, drive out demons. Freely*
> *you have received; freely give.*
>
> *⁹ "Do not get any gold or silver or copper to take*
> *with you in your belts — ¹⁰ no bag for the journey or ex-*
> *tra shirt or sandals or a staff, for the worker is worth his*
> *keep. ¹¹ Whatever town or village you enter, search there*
> *for some worthy person and stay at their house until you*
> *leave. ¹² As you enter the home, give it your greeting.*

—Matthew 10: 2–9

When I was working on a master's degree in missiology, authors such as Herbert Kane, C. Peter Wagner and Stephen Neil defined missions and missionaries in very specific categories. One was called of God, and sent by the church (normally through a mission agency) to cross boundaries (normally geographical). Upon arrival in a "new land," one would preach the gospel in pioneer areas where Jesus Christ seemed largely, if not entirely, unknown. Advocates often quoted Stephen Neil's assertion, "if everyone is a missionary then no one is a missionary." With that understanding, I would often bristle when I spoke in U.S. congregations as a missionary, hearing comments such as "everyone is a missionary." I would cringe to see the signs over the exit to the sanctuary that stated "you are now entering the mission field." How could they be missionaries? A denomination or agency did not send them as I was sent. They didn't cross the oceans as I crossed. They didn't have to live dependent upon people for offerings, and they didn't have to study culture and language like I did. How could they call them-selves missionary? In my mind, that would be like saying everyone is a pastor or an engineer.

I have struggled between this understanding of missionary and my own theological understanding of ecclesiology and mission. On one side, I understand the role of people who dedicate themselves to living incarnationally in a culture that lives very differently than their first culture. In the same way, the first century church set apart Barnabus and Paul. Similarly, God told Abraham to leave his home country and go to a place that God would direct him. So today God sends people, as part of the church, into missions. On the other side, this particular aspect of missions does not exempt the rest of the church from living into God's mission. In the 19th century, Charles Spurgeon stated "every Christian is either a missionary or an imposter."[3] Yet, as noted earlier, others stated that if everyone is a missionary, then no one is a missionary. In contrast to their view, I understand that the church "is" missionary and, as such, a sending/sent church. The real question asks not, "who is or is not a missionary?" Rather, the real question inquires "how do we live as a missionary church?"

In this short book, I challenge congregations to begin using tools similar to those used to equip individuals, but in ways that equip congregations to be missionaries. If the congregation "is" missionary, how does the congregation then live and function "as" a missionary?

HOSPITALITY, HOSTS AND GUESTS

The term "apostle" provides one of the closest biblical terms to the modern term missionary. As Jesus sent the twelve apostles, he gave them instructions to travel without extra money or resources. He also instructed them to be dependent on their hosts for housing. Some people take this very literally, and they find people who can help them when they arrive. On the other extreme, some go on mission trips by moving through a new culture from the isolation of their own rental bus and food supply; a self-contained and independent environment.

---

3. Spurgeon, "A Sermon and a Reminiscence".

The concept of reciprocity allows participants to respond to the issues raised earlier in this chapter, particularly related to guest partners who found it easier extending hospitality than receiving hospitality. A balanced model of reciprocity allows each partner to be a blessing, as well as each partner receiving a blessing from the other. The very fact that two congregations or areas work in mission together should strengthen all who participate in a partnership.

In a recent conversation with mission leaders, the question surfaced about appropriate terms used to describe U.S. congregations and their partners in other parts of the world. We discussed terms such as the sending church and the receiving church, the home church and the mission church, or the sending and host churches. Missionaries used these common terms, but we all felt that these concepts indicate a one directional and paternalistic approach to ministry. The terms represent an approach where one side sets the agenda, imposing themselves while the other partner passively receives. Many times labels and descriptors appear unimportant. In this case, they prove very important, since they describe the nature of the partnership.

As I reflect on the best practices emerging from personal research, perhaps the best terms that indicate mutuality or reciprocity in ministry includes *"host" and "guest."* When our family hosts visitors who come to stay at our home for a few days, we have an active role in providing a place for them to sleep and many times we provide meals. If new to our city, we help to orient them to the area. In a similar way, host partners play an active role as they orient their guests and come alongside guests so that their stay proves productive and helpful. Beyond the relationship, both parties in a partnership must contribute to the common mission. Paul Gupta, a mission leader in India, states "every partner must bring resources to the table. If all parties do not bring resources, it is not partnership; it is ownership."[4]

---

4. Gupta, "What the Global Church Wants the West to Know About Partnership".

The role of *guest* defines an important role in congregational partnerships. Too often, work teams and churches go to another country where they set the agenda. At times, they also form ministries and plans without consulting with their hosts, who must live with good or bad results after work teams depart. A lack of listening to the host can lead to importing expensive equipment for which the hosts cannot find parts; or raising buildings that prove out of place in the context. In some cases, medical teams might conduct a procedure only to find the host country does not possess compatible rehabilitation or follow-up mechanisms. The role of guest assumes that we reside in someone else's home, and we do not deserve the right to move furniture around, or behave like we own the place. As guests, we respect our host. Hosts know their context much better than their guests. When the guests leave, the hosts must live with long-term results.

THE DIFFERENCE BETWEEN PARENTS AND PARTNERS

This pattern demands partners intentionally strive to avoid paternalism and dependency. It also implies that relationships remain as important as ministry projects.

Food or money often frames discussions of reciprocity and trust, as mentioned earlier in this chapter. However, missiological understandings of paternalism and dependency also reflect kindred concerns that historically thwart both trust and reciprocity.

Leaders encountered these foundational challenges during the 20th century missionary movement. The majority of missions primarily emphasized transmitting the gospel, from the evangelized parts of the world to areas that had little or no Christian presence. Often missionaries, communicating the gospel to uninformed cultures, adopted a parental perspective. They viewed natives much like uninformed children, promoting a sense of developmental inferiority. These movements included ministries of compassion, but normally as secondary or peripheral to evangelism. Unfortunately compassionate activities often suffered from the same misperception, treating hurting people like children, fostering a sense of dependency rather than empowerment.

These evangelistic mission emphases still exist. They will continue to exist. However, such approaches increasingly include resources to meet humanitarian needs between two evangelized parts of the world. Missionaries should see this inclusion as a central aspect of ministry rather than a secondary aspect.

Misunderstandings in perspectives of partnership relationships seem especially evident when a partnership remains largely financial. Missiologists such as Robertson McQuilkin propose that U.S. giving often creates relationships of paternalism and unhealthy dependencies.[5] Other missiologists argue for interdependent mission relationships that include healthy financial interactions. In most partnerships, some signs appear regarding dependency and unhealthy relationships. Some would indicate that communities being served through financial support receive far more help than harm. Partnerships, however, are a recent development and these observations lack the longevity necessary to provide a better long-term assessment of congregational partnerships.

The issue of dependence remains a consistent point of concern amongst missiologists and leaders from all sides of mission work. Financial assistance remains a predominant factor in partnership relationships between U.S. congregations and churches in the majority world. Financial assistance also predominantly affects dependency. Cutting off relationships in a partnership often proves disruptive and hurtful. However, dependency creates greater challenges when leaders do not plan for transition in the relationship, which results in cutting finances.

A common strand in Western mission literature, articulated since the work of Rufus Anderson (1796-1880) and his contemporary Henry Venn (1796-1873) focused on indigenous church principles. One should note that Matthew Ricci (1552-1610) and others also practiced indigenous church principles before this time. However, Venn, Anderson, and Nevius articulation of these principles characterized the modern missionary movement. Anderson and

5 Robertson McQuilkin *Stop Sending Money!*

Venn addressed issues of indigeneity by exploring broader aspects of the developing church in new areas. Still, indigenous church principles retained the belief churches should behave consistently with their local culture. This behavior (known as the three "selfs") included finances, decision making, and the ability to evangelize within their own culture, all without dependency on outside agencies. John Nevius applied indigenous principles as an attempt to avoid financial dependency. Nevius wasn't against the use of outside funds for missionary work. However, he felt, "the injudicious use of money and agencies depending on money have retarded and crippled our work and produced a less self-reliant and stalwart type of Christian than we otherwise should have had."[6]

Robertson McQuilkin provides a contemporary voice expressing similar concerns as those of Nevius. Glenn Schwartz makes similar arguments against dependency and paternalism in his 1994 article titled "Cutting the Apron Stings" in *Evangelical Mission Quarterly*. One should note McQuilkin, as well as Schwartz, primarily address traditional church planting initiatives rather than partnerships between two congregations.

Nevius' perspective, alongside many others since then, calls for independence and self- sufficiency. The approach appears consistent with the understanding that the task of mission involves church planting around a centralized mission organization. This focus proves consistent with Robert Schreiter's definition of the second wave of mission mentioned in chapter one. This model, however, proves challenging, particularly in an environment that views the mission of the church

> (N)ot solely a movement from spaces where there are Christians to spaces where there are not, but rather a movement from spaces where there are Christians and churches that have extensive material resources to other spaces where there are significant numbers of Christians and churches that live under circumstances of material poverty and social constraint.[7]

6. Nevious, *Planting and Developing of Missionary Churches*, 8.

7. Priest, *A New Era of Mission is Upon Us*, 297.

Without a doubt, issues of giving, dependency, and poverty remain just as vital (if not more so) within this changing framework of the third wave of mission.

The second wave concentrated on planting churches to establish the gospel. Nevius' global context included planters focused on pioneer mission work in new areas.

In the current global context, mission also includes former pioneer areas of the 20th century. These areas include growing and developing three-self churches. These same areas now face epidemic crises such as HIV/AIDS, and natural disasters like earthquakes, tsunamis, and drought. Many ministers contend adherence to McQuilkin's or Schwartz's approach to normal church development, in the face of such global human suffering, proves damaging to the church's testimony. However, those who adhere to relationship-over-structure do not accept the maxim, "just send money," without a relationship. The challenge in our current society, therefore, requires quality relationships. These relationships ideally take questions of paternalism and dependency seriously while learning healthy financial models in the context of financial disparity.

Issues of dependency and financial aid in Africa remain a topic of sharp critique in popular and academic writing. Books that illustrate the critique include Dambisa Moyo's *Dead Aid* and Easterly's *White Man's Burden*. Moyo's thesis asserts the countries of Africa who benefited from the greatest financial aid appear no better off, but worse from the support. Moyo offers a solution of development in Africa without dependence on foreign aid. Urbanologist Robert Lupton makes a similar argument by stating charity efforts often become destructive instead of helpful. Lupton, who addresses aid to the U.S. urban societies, remains sharply critical of U.S. church efforts. Yet Lupton offers a solution that seems less extreme than Moyo's. Lupton's solution appears, in many ways, consistent with those who state that quality relationships remain key. In *Toxic Charity*, Lupton encourages churches to redirect their efforts away from destructive patterns of compassion. He steers congregations toward thoughtful paths toward community development.

The financial assistance challenge between U.S. and African partners revolves around the issue of quality relationships where one takes time to listen and learn from the other. When participants define "quality relationships" as relationships where each partner hears and learns from the other, simple answers such as "just send money," or "don't send money," do not apply. David Marantz's book, *African Friends and Money Matters*, demonstrates how Africans and Westerners think of money quite differently. Superficial business relationships do not understand the different economic systems. Rather, quality relationships seek to hear and understand one another.

Ironically, the current setting includes a desire for relation alongside an environment of short-term mission encounters that limit interaction between two cultures. The quality relationships that do occur reflect primarily bonding social capital relationships between members of the short-term mission team. Still, the growing phenomenon of short-term missions provides an example of churches who prefer active involvement in building relationships, rather than "just sending money" to mission agencies or the mission field.

One could argue that people don't want to give funds to an organization. So the impetus for partnership may simply come out of a desire to be a participant donor, and to help distant, needy people. Relationships that remain heavily dependent on donors affect how congregations frame the "other." Advocates, seeking to secure funds, often provide stories, and portray images, that frame people in the host country. These narratives and images depict the enormous difference between the donor and the recipient by using pictures to demonstrate bleak situations of extreme poverty. The October 2002 issue of the *International Bulletin of Missionary Research* examined this very problem. The journal demonstrated the stereotyping and sensationalism often appears evident through missionary photography. Compounded with the need for raising funds, John Hutnyk, in his book *The Rumour of Calcutta*, describes how tourists often frame an image of a location such as Calcutta before they visit. Tourists often take pictures of things that reinforce how they framed the location before going. For example, should the person frame Calcutta in terms of poverty, he or she often takes pictures that reinforce poverty, even when surrounded by other possible images. In short-term mission (STM) or Congregational Partnerships, images brought back from the experience, and shown to congregations, often emphasize the "otherness." While a blurred line between donor and recipient serves as an ideal, the enormous need for financing through emotional appeals makes that ideal a challenge. The danger rests with forming relationships that reinforce boundaries of "otherness" instead of relationships with blurred boundaries.

Balancing between relationship and project remains a challenge, one that may not completely blur the line between donor and recipient. However, quality relationships that seek to hear and understand the other provide a common denominator in STM and congregational mission research literature. These relationships serve as a necessary basis for healthy cross-cultural partnerships.

HEALTHY RELATIONSHIPS

A number of theories undergird the models of relationship provided in this chapter. Anthropologist, Muneo Yoshikawa typology of cross-cultural relationships provides a helpful tool to understand the nature of partnership relations. Yoshikawa describes a double-swing model for intercultural communication, one based on Martin Buber's concept of a dialogical relationship.[8] Yoshikawa describes four categories of cross-cultural relationships: ethnocentric, control mode, dialectic mode, and dialogical mode. Other theorists draw from this work to describe partnership relationships. Philip Thomas' article in the *International Review of Missions* serves as a great example.[9] Thomas presents his typology as a progressive movement from one-direction relationships to transformative relationships. The most effective relationships in

8. Buber, *I and Thou.*

9. Thomas, "How Can Western Christians Learn From Patterns in the World Church?"

Thomas' typology include reciprocity, with mutual learning and exchange (similar to Yoshikawa's dialogical model). Nelson, King and Smith, in their book *Going Global*, draw on the typology to describe congregational partnership relationships. One might understand some surveyed partnerships within the framework of this typology. In the Swaziland Partnership, however, one does not find a linear progression from one level to another. These typologies exist simultaneously. The Swaziland Partnership appears interactive, with more than just two cultures or two entities. Relationships prove more complex than simply describing culture "A" engaging culture "B." Nevertheless, these categories serve as a helpful framework for describing the nature of partnership relationships between congregations.

During the research of the Bethany First/Swaziland Partnership, those from Bethany First Church worked to dialog and listen to those in Swaziland. Participants stated several times, both in Swaziland as well as in Oklahoma, the objective remained to do things with, not for, the Swazis. Nevertheless, participants often understood these ideals quite differently in the process of a large, financially strong, congregation in Oklahoma partnering with multiple structures in Swaziland toward a common mission.

One could title the first model the sponsorship approach, or ethnocentric approach, or directive approach, or control approach. One might also simply call it a one-directional approach since communication remains one-sided.

FIGURE 1: SPONSORSHIP RELATIONSHIP MODEL

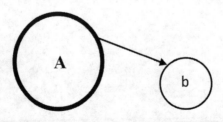

An extreme example of this approach entails Partner A devising strategies while ignoring or overlooking partner B, not asking for input. One reason for this condescension could include ethnocentrism; dominant partners do not feel that the other partner proves equally capable. A milder version of this approach surfaces when partner A asks questions and asks for input, but only as a matter of courtesy, discounting partner B's view. This model also surfaces when participants ask questions and expect feedback without considering cultural differences. So partner A interprets responses through their own cultural understanding. Overall, in this model, partners ignore culture and omit effective methods for feedback. Stated differently, often people don't realize that another set of cultural assumptions seems even possible. Rather than ignoring what should be obvious, no brief visitor can realistically be expected to grasp another's cultural viewpoint.

A gift given to Swaziland pastors by a U.S. guest provides example of the cultural gap. Bill (pseudonym used) possessed good intentions, using his abilities in art to encourage Swazi pastors. Bill consulted with the cultural brokers to translate the bible verse into Siswati; *ingelese ka Jehova; ngenisa inxa zonke kwabamesabayo ba kulute Amahube* (The angel of the Lord encamps around those who fear him, and he delivers them. –Psalm 34:7

Figure 2: Painting of Angel and Pastor

The artist intended to encourage the pastors by depicting a Swazi pastor, in the midst of challenges, protected by an angel. The painting shows angry lions around the pastor and a large angel with a halo, white skin, and large wings protecting the pastor from the lions. The artist depicted the pastor with black skin and diminutive in relation to the angel.

Those from BFC framed Swazis and themselves, seeing the Swazi pastors being surrounded by the challenges of AIDS and poverty. Bill intended to encourage the pastors, communicating that God's presence remained with them even in these challenges.

The picture could be interpreted in a variety of ways. On the surface level, for those from BFC and possibly for some from Swaziland the picture communicated Bill's intent. An African understanding of the culture, however, might lead to a very different interpretation. Within the context of Africa, artwork often depicts deity with white skin similar to the colonializers. In an African setting this well-meaning gift could represent a paternalistic interpretation of the white protectors, with an unintended result generating hurtful and divisive feelings. The artist did seek to contextualize the painting by translating the verse and painting the pastor with black skin. Unfortunately the artist, who was in Africa for a short time, however, did not have sufficient background that allowed him to perceive how an African would interpret the painting.

Sponsorship, instead of a partnership, provides a more accurate way to describe this model (see the section "types of partnerships" in chapter one). The approach implies partner A sponsors the ministry of partner B. In other settings partner B may actually sponsor partner A by providing a venue for visitors to have a short-term mission experience.

Although not the predominant model of the partnerships I surveyed, some aspects of this model seemed present in most of them. In some cases the lead pastor (and/or partnership coordinator) from the guest church intentionally asked for input from those in the host location. In the best cases, those from the guest church have intentionally worked to avoid seeming overbearing. Cultural distinctiveness, however, reflects a blind spot which people do not always take into consideration. Guests often hear "yes" answers when they bring a pre-developed plan. Such responses often happen in meetings with strict time schedules. Interviewed Swazis stated they wished that they could plan in more relaxed situations, over a period, so they could discuss plans without pressure.

Guests and hosts encounter challenges to the relationship when guests perceive some projects as very important, but not so for those in the host location. In some partnerships, those from the guest church hear their host and discontinued their plans. In other cases, however, guests persist with projects even when host leadership wants to take a different direction. Examples include projects popular in the U.S., such as orphanages or child development centers. U.S. churches can raise funds for these types of projects, and many people have an interest in helping children. However, the host may express that efforts like orphanages inappropriately separate children from the community. This stance challenges the guest ministry to work toward a common understanding of the problem, and then a common approach to the solution.

A second model, more reflective of many relationships within congregational partnerships, proves similar to what Nelson, King and Smith[10] call an instructive model:

FIGURE 3: INSTRUCTIVE RELATIONSHIP MODEL

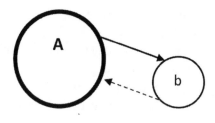

10. Nelson et al., Going Global, 113.

In this model, partner A listens to partner b; and Partner A understands the needs of partner b, but partner A remains the dominant partner, and they work from their own cultural perspective. The elephant and mouse story mentioned earlier illustrates the problem, where the elephant and the mouse dance together, and the elephant means well, but the mouse gets squashed.

A farm project on one partnership provided one example. The guest church listened to their host express a need to support theology students. The guest church also listened to hosts who said they thought that a farm at their seminary might serve the need. The guest heard the need, and they heard the desire of the host friends. Guests translated perceived needs and desires into a business plan; one developed according to good U.S., business practices before being brought back to the host for 'buy in." When it came to finalizing the business plan, the negative reaction by the host church surprised those from the guest church. The guest thought that they were responding to the needs and the ideas of the host. However, the host church responded both to the dominance of the guest partner in the project, and fear of losing control of the project.

A major question related to this model surfaced: "who sets the agenda?" Vital questions included, "Who sets the itinerary for the visiting teams? Who makes decisions for accepting or rejecting projects? Who sets the standard for the use of funds? Who makes the menu for common meals?" To a large degree, most partnerships include mutual dialog and understanding between host and guest, but normally the guest ultimately sets the agenda.

This model of instructive relationship proves helpful in the sense that the U.S. partner at least assesses the real needs and listens to the real concerns of their host partner. However, the model demonstrates risks as the dominance of one partner limits benefits of the partnership by short cutting the mutual exchange of knowledge and experience. Moving beyond this model proves challenging in partnerships focused on a series of short-term teams.

A third model, the Transformational Relationship Model reflects the nature of some partnerships. This model appears similar to what Yoshikawa calls a dialectic mode, or what others call a dialogical or transformational mode. Yoshikawa's draws from Buber's work *I and Thou.* Yoshikawa states "Buber became more concerned with the dialogical unity which emphasizes the act of meeting between two different beings without eliminating the otherness or uniqueness of each."[11] This meeting, according to Buber, sharpens the uniqueness of each partner.

FIGURE 4: TRANSFORMATIONAL RELATIONSHIP MODEL

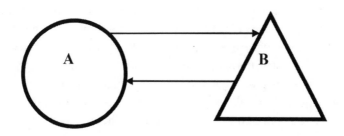

This model proves challenging since no real comfortable space exists to ignore the contradictions and challenges of each other partner. The realities that create challenges entail a paradoxical form of unity. Buber illustrates the paradox using alternatives like love and justice, or the love of God and the fear of God. To a certain extent, the model represents the ideal, or hoped for, outcome of partnerships expressed in many of the interviews.

The farm project demonstrates not only the instructive model, but retains aspects of the dialogical model as host leaders spoke up and addressed the aggressiveness of the guest church. Those from the guest church heard them and made adjustments in which both parties learned from each other and the final result reflected input from both sides.

11. Yoshikawa, "The Double-Swing Model of Intercultural Communication Between the East and the West," 323.

Yoshikawa's fourth model, the double swing model, describes a form of the dialogical model, yet goes beyond humanitarian aid. The model moves toward a solidarity that mutually transforms both sides into something greater than the sum of the two. In the first ethnocentric model, b remains a mere shadow of A. In the second instructional model A dominates b and b proves useful to A as only a means to achieve A's purposes. The third, dialectic model recognizes the differences of both parties and works toward hearing, understanding and acknowledging those differences. A fourth model occurs when "A's thesis is met by B's antithesis, and creates a new synthesis which proves unique and transcends the differences of A and B which are lost in C."[12]

FIGURE 5: DIALOGICAL RELATIONSHIP MODEL

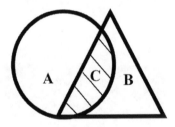

Some have described this synthesis as blurring the lines between donor and recipient as two congregations work interdependently.

In a mission framework that focuses on a relationship, it must be noted that not all relationships have the same level of quality. Challenges of patronage and exploitation are nearly always evident in these types of relationships. Given that grassroots networks formed many of these partnerships, rather than agency or denominational oversight, the phenomenon remains unpredictable.

This changing approach to mission challenges denominations and mission agencies. Frankly the approach challenges all

12. Ibid, 320.

mission structures (including educational structures) to make an important shift in how they relate to congregations. These organizations traditionally serve as "gatekeepers," in contrast to the third wave framework. They need to negotiate with the networks of partnerships in order to strengthen relationships instead of controlling them. In this sense, therefore, partnerships exist between more than two congregations. Partnerships also include a platform organization, such as a mission structure. While discussed further in chapter six, the need for reciprocity between all participants, and the need for a move away from hierarchal structures to mutual partnerships of trust and accountability, proves essential for healthy partnerships.

4

Communicating the Mission

You need a guide to have cultural intelligence. You can't just work it all out by yourself no matter how smart you are; no matter how observant you are you need a Swazi guide.

—Michaele Lavigne, cultural broker in Swaziland

A third common pattern of healthy partnerships works intentionally toward clear, quality communication between all involved in the partnership. This pattern implies consistent, open communication that builds trust. A further implication suggests the need for cultural brokers who can navigate communication. More than any other factor, the role of a cultural broker serves as the most essential aspect of healthy and effective congregational partnerships. The cultural broker's ability to bridge various parts of a partnership often determines the success or failure of a partnership.

COMMUNICATION THAT BUILDS TRUST

Among the congregations that I spoke with for this study, churches developed a variety of systems for good communication with their ministry partners. Some partnerships ran into obstacles due to false expectations from congregants who could leverage funds and aggressively address perceived needs. Others ran into obstacles due to false expectations from their ministry partners. Nearly all of the partnerships faced the challenge of needing someone who understood both sides of the partnership. Someone who could interface or broker between those involved.

A congregation may easily misinterpret expectations when not accustomed to the complexities of cross-cultural communication. Effective cross-cultural communication that takes into account each side of the partnership requires skilled and thoughtful mediators or brokers. The development of this role is perhaps the greatest need as well as the greatest challenge in the ongoing development of healthy partnerships.

This chapter introduces the vital role of the cultural broker in healthy partnerships. We begin with a description of the term cultural broker. A case study of the cultural brokers in Swaziland/Bethany First Church partnership provides an example of one congregation's development of the role. This chapter reviews the variety of cultural brokers, from those in challenging areas of the world, to brokers residing in small congregations. Organizations such as relief organizations provide a final example of cultural brokers. The chapter concludes by offering common best practices within all of these examples.

THE ROLE OF CULTURAL BROKERS

I have hesitated to use the title "cultural brokers" since it carries connotations of a U.S. business model that can be easily misinterpreted by different cultural understandings. When I have used this term, people from outside the U.S. frequently offer suggestions to replace the term *broker* with terms such as mediator, connector, bridge builder, or interface. I borrowed the term "broker" from Kersten Bayt Priest's research of Christian women engaged in short-term mission travel. Priest uses the term "resource broker" to describe how women visit areas of great need in Africa and, on behalf of the needs, begin to broker to work associates and businesses in the U.S. The women organized events and gathered resources on behalf of their friends in Africa.

Priest develops the concept of cultural broker, stating, "cultural brokers understand enough about not only their own culture, but also the culture of traveling missioners –at least within the interactional space of the short-term trip 'contact zone.'"[1] Since Priests' research focuses primarily on short-term contacts, the cultural broker often acts as a tour guide with language skills. An American missionary, or a highly resourced national, usually serves as a broker. Priest's understanding of this concept proves helpful but does not carry the full intention of a cultural broker for congregational partnerships.

I use the term "cultural broker" since it does include an aspect of someone who understands a culture on both sides of the partnership. Participants outside of the U.S., and those from partner congregations, help sharpen this concept. In congregational partnerships, the cultural broker serves as a mediator. One who interprets for both sides in a balanced manner, and clarifies often misunderstood issues. Some readers may interpret this role as someone who does not particularly carry forward their own agenda. Readers may assume the broker only helps to bridge or interface between two sides. Cultural brokers, however, do not simply remain unbiased interpreters. They also help both sides understand the broader issues. This understanding turns projects away from unhealthy mission practices toward healthy ones.

Unlike the tour guide model, the cultural broker for congregational partnerships should have sufficient theological and missiological understanding. This understanding guides projects toward the ultimate purpose of God's mission within a cross-cultural context. Understanding the interrelationship between ecclesiology (the church), and mission in a context, gives the cultural broker a balanced view. This view guides the effectiveness of the partnership.

1. Kerstyn Priest, *Caring for the Least of These: Christian Women's Short-Term Mission Travel*, 55.

CASE STUDIES OF THE CULTURAL BROKER

As a new partnership formed between Bethany First Church and Swaziland, the U.S. church made an early decision to place cultural brokers for their congregation in Swaziland.[2] These volunteers served in Swaziland for one year as on-site representatives of the congregation's missions pastor. The church's website stated, "on-site coordinators were needed to build relationships and to work the partnership.[3]" The church first chose a retired couple; they left Swaziland early due to a medical emergency. Couples aging from the 20's to early 30's served as the next four cultural brokers. They possessed limited intercultural education and cross-cultural ministry provided a new experience.

Observers should note the unique pattern for both the church and the denomination. A local Nazarene congregation selects, prepares, and sends its own missionaries, instead of commissioning them through the denominational mission agency. These couples do attend a three-day volunteer orientation conducted by the denomination's department of Global Mission. However, the local church selects and primarily trains the couples.

Alongside several cultural broker interviews, I talked with a couple that reported that they went to Swaziland with instructions to be the "ears and eyes" for their church in Swaziland. They also served as a representative of BFC to the Swazis. During the process, the couple reported that they saw their allegiance shift a bit. They realized there was a greater need to understand the Swazi partners and advocate for them back at BFC. One couple observed, "You really do need a guide to have cultural intelligence. You can't just work it all out by yourself no matter how smart you are, no matter how observant you are, you need a Swazi guide." All of the cultural broker couples reported how doors opened for them as they acknowledged their respect for Swazi guidance.

2. Note that this church uses the term *on-site coordinator* for this role. I used the term *cultural broker* to describe the position

3. http://www.swazipartners.org/the-beginning (accessed December 8, 2011).

A pastor's AIDS conference scheduled in Swaziland served as an example. The initial planning for the Pastor's conference began at BFC. The church leadership asked, "What is going to change the tide of the HIV epidemic in Swaziland?" The cultural brokers said "the chatter was amongst ourselves [at BFC] as we asked, 'what's the best idea that we can present to the Swazis?'" The broker, however, said that she felt uneasy with who was answering the question. She decided to talk to pastors and ministry leaders in Swaziland. The cultural broker described the process:

> Swazi conversation can kind of take a while and especially if they think I have something I'm trying to get at. So, I tried really hard to craft questions and listen and take time and then find a back door to say, well might it look something like this, or did you have something else in mind? Through those conversations then, [we found] they totally know what they need and they know what's going to turn the tide. And it was really this kind of ah-ha moment of wow, we're working so hard to try to figure it out and we just had to ask them what they already knew.

As a result, brokers worked on preparing a proposal that took these ideas and concerns of the Swazis into account. This proposal expressed the format and length of the conference that the Swazis wanted. Instead of the U.S. church paying for everything, the Swazis proposed that Americans provide some of the resources. However, the Swazis provided resources as well. The change proved a turning point in the partnership according to the cultural brokers. Swazis who attended the conference paid for most of their own costs, unlike other conferences between U.S. churches and Swazis. The U.S. church also contributed additional funds for their participation. The presenters at the conference included three Africans and three North Americans. The hosts of the conference were four church leaders from Swaziland. Swazis stated they needed to know they were not facing the challenge of AIDS alone. Pastors stated that they needed practical ways to address the AIDS epidemic. The need surfaced in their congregations, where so many people, whether infected or indirectly affected by AIDS, rarely discussed the issue.

The role of the cultural brokers between the U.S. church and Swaziland provides a vital component to the health of the Swaziland Partnership. When questioned, those in Swaziland overwhelmingly appreciate the couples' presence. From the Swazi perspective, the cultural broker's position of dependency on Swazi leadership proves healthy. The dependency allows a balanced partnership between the U.S. congregation and Swaziland.

The profiles of the four couples from this congregation proved diverse. They included a retired couple, a newly wedded couple just graduating from university, and couples in their late twenties. The skills of the coordinators included construction, computer technology, pastoral ministry, and business education. The couples seemed similar since they possessed little missions' education or experience (other than one couple that took minimal missions course work in college). A common characteristic surfaced in the couples' flexibility toward the needs of leaders in Swaziland, and the needs of the U.S. church. All of the couples went to Swaziland without knowledge of *Siswati*, and for the majority of their time they remained heavily dependent on Swazis. The pattern required all couples to build good relations with Swazis, and work with the churches in Swaziland between short-term team visits. The cultural brokers would preach in churches, assist areas of their expertise, and gain a better understanding of the needs of Swaziland. They would also broker between the U.S. congregation and Swaziland, often dialoging regularly with the U. S. missions pastor as they prepared for short-term teams. When teams arrive, they work with the mission pastor to coordinate the activities of the teams.

Bethany First Church members didn't perceive their cultural brokers as short-term volunteers. Members described brokers in the same manner as previous long-term missionaries; who sacrificially left everything behind for a lifetime of service. Parishioners hold cultural brokers in high esteem. Brokers live as role models to the children and youth of the church, speaking in services and participating in the guest church after their year in Swaziland.

The cultural brokers begin their year as volunteers when they go to Swaziland in the summer. They fly back to the U.S. for Christmas and then return to Swaziland for the rest of their year. When in the U.S., the brokers report to the church and spend vacation time with their families. In the interviews at the U.S. church, people referred to the cultural brokers as their missionaries. Congregants spoke of the sacrifices that the brokers had to make to be in Swaziland for the year. Those at the church mention how the cultural brokers pack up their things in the U.S. and place them in storage, quit good jobs, sell houses and cars. Several of those interviewed feel that the stress of living a full year in Swaziland proves overbearing. They offered solutions to address the difficulty.

Overwhelmingly, people at Bethany First Church acknowledge the essential role of the cultural brokers in building relationships in Swaziland. The relationships help the short-term mission teams serve more effectively. The cultural brokers also gain the favor of the leaders in Swaziland by respecting local leadership and existing ecclesial structure.

A ministry leader in Swaziland spoke positively about the cultural brokers. The leader reported, "they are the hands on people, and you know, I don't think, let me be careful in what I'm saying, I don't think that this partnership would really mean anything or go somewhere without those volunteers. I will go as far as saying that."

I questioned Swaziland participants if it would be better to have career missionaries in this position. Career missionaries serve as representatives of the denomination instead of one local church. Participants responded having current missionaries serving as volunteers from Bethany First Church places them in a positive relationship in Swaziland. Missionaries serving in the role of volunteer provided a non-hierarchical relation, a position of equal partners. This perspective may speak more to the need to change the role of the missionary. However, the perspective also points to the need of those in the cultural broker role to take a posture of partnership instead of the role of director or control.

Cultural brokers provide an important part of both good health and positive relationships within the Swaziland Partnership. Their insight into the Swaziland Partnership also proves important. Asked what had been learned thus far in the partnership, one cultural broker responded:

> I think that you could start smaller. Have less ambitious goals. Not that goals are a bad thing, but they make Americans antsy if it is taking too long and that makes us push because we want to have something to report when World Mission Sunday comes back around.

Three of the four couples felt that a two-year time frame was better than one year for the on-site coordinators to be in Swaziland. In response to this extension, one couple said "If the onsite coordinator is only there to get stuff done on the ground, then a year is fine, but if the on-site coordinator is there to get to the level of relationships that we were able to start getting at and make the partnership more on a friendship level then I think it has to be longer."

OTHER EXAMPLES OF CULTURAL BROKERS

The nature of the relationship, and the people involved, nuance any relationship. Congregational partnerships appear no different. The partnership between Bethany First Church and Swaziland remains unique to their situations. Likewise, one finds a variety of forms depicting the role of cultural broker. Partnerships occur in different global contexts. Congregations that engage in partnerships remain diverse. Some assumed that partnerships appear limited to mega-churches with resources, such as Bethany First. Partnerships, however, occur in churches that are small as well as large. I have found partnerships in churches of 50, 150, 800 as well as 10,000 members. Partnerships exist in denominational just as they do in independent churches. Every congregation interviewed possessed some form of a cultural broker, although each church context, and each host partner shaped the relationship each partnership.

Perhaps the most complex and challenging partnerships occur in congregations with partnerships in countries where an official missionary or cultural broker is not allowable. These challenges often include restrictions on email and social media, as well as language differences. In one case, the country remains favorable toward different groups coming into the country to construct clinics and churches. The cultural broker for this partnership may include a group of people rather than an individual. The host country has a person who coordinates their side of the partnership and helps determine potential projects. The guest congregation appoints a person in their church, primarily because of their language abilities. The guest broker communicates the requests of the host country, and communicates short-term mission team plans back to the guest congregation. This represents a new partnership yet taking form. However, at this early stage it represents a model of serial short-term mission trips focusing on a specific location.

In another instance, the partnership resides in a large Asian country. This beginning partnership requires working to find a good way to form clear communication in a complex situation. The communication proves crucial when it appears difficult to show measurable results to the congregation, like buildings or evangelistic events. It seems equally difficult to establish on-going communication with their partners. This congregation possesses one unique aspect. The lead pastor also maintains a leadership role in the host country, and currently serves in the role of cultural broker. In both examples, the magnified complexities of communication necessitate skilled cultural brokers to form healthy relationships.

Beyond these two illustrations, other churches work with career missionaries. A church in Oklahoma City, in a partnership in Zambia, works with a career missionary in that country who serves as their primary cultural broker. This missionary has lived in Zambia for many years. The missionary knows the culture in-depth and works to lift up Zambian leadership in every step of the partnership. Beyond the local cultural knowledge, the missionary communicates well with the participating U.S. congregation, and does not hesitate to correct cultural misunderstandings. The mission pastor of this church stated they realize that their church's role remains short-term in nature. So the missionary serves as a bridge to the longer mission of Zambia. "We do not drive the bus," said the mission pastor, "we are just along for the ride".

What proves key to this particular partnership is the missionary understanding his role as a broker between the Oklahoma City Church and Zambia. Perhaps this example represents an ideal broker in most situations. The position, however, defines a challenging role for missionaries. Missionaries who reside in a country long enough to truly understand the culture often see the work of U.S. churches as a distraction to the "real work" of missions. Or they see the U.S. churches only serving a role in funding their ministry. Missionaries also run the risk of allowing visiting U.S. churches full reign in activities, just to make the visitors happy. The result generates a great risk of paternal practices toward local leadership in the host location, or creating the risk of dependency. However, in this particular case, the missionary serves as a broker with a long term trajectory of the church in mind. Also, the missionary works to minister to the U.S church by including them in the process.

One can describe Jacob's Well Church, in Kansas City, as a non-denominational, missionary minded church of approximately 700 people. Jacob's Well maintains a partnership with a congregation in Kenya in order to install water wells. This partnership emerged in an organic manner. The lead pastor of Jacobs Well, together with a leadership group, met a Kenyan pastor at a conference. They spoke about their common desire to provide water wells for people in rural areas of Kenya. Together, these two congregations began working in a third location in order to install water wells. This partnership appears unique since the Kenya partner does not "receive" the mission efforts. Rather, the partnership involves a U. S. congregation, and a congregation in Nairobi, Kenya, working together in a common mission to a third location. The cultural broker in this case serves as the lead pastor of the church in Nairobi. This pastor interfaces between rural communities, his congregation, and Jacob's Well. This partnership requires a great deal of trust. In this example, it works because the cultural broker is a trusted person who is not the recipient of the funds.

NGO'S AND ASSISTANCE ORGANIZATIONS AS CULTURAL BROKERS

Instead of relying on a cultural broker from their congregation, or individuals in the host location, some larger congregations turn to assistance organizations like *Compassion International* to broker the relationships. The organization assists congregations as they engage in large-scale issues such as human trafficking, water initiatives, gender based violence, etc. In some congregations interviewed, this relationship appeared very positive. I will describe one of these relationships in more detail in chapter 5. In other instances, however, congregations stated some organizations did not act as a neutral mediator. In worst case scenarios, organizations worked to build their own sponsorship base from the congregations. The organizations withheld excess funds for their own use. Also, these organizations often maintained their own agenda instead of mediating between the guest and host partners. If a congregation chooses to utilize this form of organization as a cultural broker, it should clearly define expectations and communication as the partnership begins.

All of the partnerships included some form of cultural broker. However, most congregations expressed the need to develop this role further in order to improve communication and mission development. A common thread amongst partnerships asserts the need for effective ways to prepare cultural brokers or link to those who can serve as cultural brokers. Organizations that meet this need in thoughtful ways serve one of the greatest needs for healthy congregational partnership[4].

4. Camino Del Red represents one organization that works with the role of cultural broker; led by Dee and Tom Yaccino. Their website is http://www. delcaminoconnection.org/list/category/reflections-and-resources

SOME BEST PRACTICES FOR CULTURAL BROKERS

Based on the various partnerships, some common themes emerge with cultural brokers. These themes incorporate "best practices" that may help any congregation insure clear, quality communication to foster the mission of the partnership through these brokers.

1. The cultural broker fills a vital role in any congregational partnership that includes parties geographically distant from one another. Conversely, although a vital role, cultural brokers remain underdeveloped and require needed attention. The need provides an opportunity for congregations, mission agencies, and education providers as they collaboratively facilitate those in the role of cultural broker. Educational providers, such as seminaries with missiology related programs, occupy a unique position. Often these providers use many missiological tools in conjunction with congregational studies methods to offer focused certificate or degree programs. The programs give the cultural broker a foundation for their unique position of ministry. Mission agencies traditionally focused on missionaries as church planters, mission administrators, or short-term mission coordinators. These agencies should make a place for missionaries who intentionally see their role in partnerships as a ministry to the global context where they live. This role goes beyond moving resources in one direction and toward quality mutual relationships that focus on God's mission.

2. The cultural broker's capacity to build relationships through learning language and culture proves essential. While there is value in having a humble posture, there is also a need for the person/people to go beyond the surface of the host culture. Similarly, if the cultural broker seems more familiar with the host culture, he, or she must learn the language and culture of the guest partner. This learning proves necessary in order to mediate, or interface adequately, for sustained projects and objectives. The need implies the cultural broker becomes a student of at least two distinct contexts.

3. Cultural Brokers with some missiological education enhance their ability to recognize aspects of dependency, reciprocity, and paternalism. These aspects often weaken the good intentions of the partnership. Education could also help to build healthy models that enhance the efforts of the partnership. Knowledge provides a great asset to congregations, as well as to a host location. This knowledge helps to assure that their efforts result in a long-term, healthy impact on the host location as well as their congregation.

4. Cultural brokers should contribute to the long term planning and decisions related to the partnership in the host country. In some cases, the cultural brokers maintain no active role other than carrying out the objectives of the guest partner. In other instances the broker serves as a source of income or resources for the host, but demonstrates no interest in ministering to the guest partner. However, the cultural broker should enhance the decisions made on both sides of the partnership. These decisions ultimately lead to long term, healthy mission development.

The cultural broker provides a new role for missionaries. Congregations, mission agencies, and seminaries should prioritize any effort that strengthens this role. Strong, healthy partnerships necessitate intentional efforts that develop people who can navigate the complexities of cross-cultural partnerships.

5

The Church as Missionary

"The Church then intentionally bears witness to the meaning and relevance of the kingdom, while not itself being identical with that kingdom. It is called to the risky task of being the living interpretation of that kingdom; otherwise, the kingdom can be little more than a slogan, ideology of human programme of betterment"

—LESSLIE NEWBIGIN, SIGN OF THE KINGDOM [1]

I dream of a "missionary option," that is, a missionary impulse capable of transforming everything, so that the Church's customs, ways of doing things, times and schedules, language and structures can be suitably channeled for the evangelization of today's world rather than for her self-preservation.

—POPE FRANCIS 2014 ADDRESS TO THE BISHOPS AND CLERGY. [2]

---

1. *Newbigin, Sign of the Kingdom 1980, 19*
2. Francis, *Apostolic Exhortation Evangelii Guadium 2014, 25*

"We are forced to do something that the Western churches have never had to do since the days of their own birth-to discover the form and substance of a missionary church in terms that are valid in a world that has rejected the power and the influence of the Western nation."

—LESSLIE NEWBIGIN, THE OPEN SECRET 1995[3]

A FOURTH COMMON PATTERN of healthy partnerships occurs when healthy partnerships focuses on God's mission. Possessing this general theological vision implies connecting partnership activities to local mission involvement. The vision also implies an intentional effort to help participants integrate their experience with their work and life.

GOD'S MISSION MATTERS

This chapter reveals the essential nature of Christianity as mission. Swazi women who serve those dying of HIV/AIDs related illnesses demonstrate an expression of Christian identity rather than a program of the church. In like manner, this chapter attests to a theological understanding of the mission of God as the essential nature of the church in which church is the missionary or a missionary ecclesiology. In opposition to a utilitarian view of mission that makes decisions based on simply what works, the chapter draws from the work of missiologists such as David Bosch and Lesslie Newbigin to establish that healthy partnerships work toward a broader view of mission. Rather than limit missionary activity to one or two week trips to a distant land, mission partnerships include every aspect of the church and the life of the Christian. Practical examples of various churches provide a guide of best practices that direct a congregation toward a self-understanding of the church as missionary.

3. Newbigin, The Open Secret 1995, 5

CHRISTIAN IDENTITY THROUGH
A LENTEN EXPERIENCE

I was in Swaziland during most of the season of Lent, and some-how that seemed both fitting and unfitting at the same time. It ap-peared fitting, not because I felt compelled to give up things (other than my family) in order to be there, but because I witnessed a very Christian tradition of bearing another's burden.

For a week, I went on home visits with the *Swaziland HIV/ AIDS Task Force*. I traveled with founders, Mary Magagula and Evelyn Shongwe, who work with almost 200 volunteer team care-givers providing home-based care to those dying of AIDS. The Task Force encourages communities to form co-ops for gardens. They also support 95 children through child sponsorship. Mary and Evelyn, along with other Christians in Swaziland, saw those in need around them. They then simply decided to find ways to live out their faith.

One morning, upon arriving at the task force office, I dis-covered seven large (and very heavy) nylon bags as part of what we took to each home. Each bag contained large bags of meale, peanuts, beans, rice and cooking oil. The bags contain staple, transportable, products easily prepared, and, according to Evelyn, with high nutritional value. I helped load the bags into the back of the 4X4 truck, and we headed toward the area where we would make home visits.

After a 30-minute drive on pavement, we arrived at a mar-ginalized community on the mountainside of Manzini. We left the paved surface, turning onto a deeply rutted dirt road for a ride resembling a bucking bronco. At points, the ruts proved extremely deep, and the heavy vegetation made the roads very narrow. Ev-elyn and Mary pointed out the extreme difficulty reaching these communities by vehicle. People struggling with severe illnesses find it even more difficult to leave in order to find medical help.

The first home we visited entailed a cement structure with a tin roof. A two to three-year-old girl greeted us in the doorway with a frilly red dress torn in several places and a very runny nose.

The same dynamic presented itself in every home we visited. All homes included people who contend with the process of dying soon under difficult circumstances. In many cases, they must leave their children in the care of grandmothers. In every case, Evelyn appeared like a light coming into a dark room. She possesses a jovial spirit with which she brought sincere and appropriate laughter to these situations.

As we entered the house, I noticed the cement walls with peeling paint and wires hanging loose at all of the electrical outlets. However, the house appeared incredibly clean and well kept. Near the door lay the woman that we came to visit. She tested HIV positive and also suffered from tuberculosis (that was the case in nearly all visits that we made). She lay on the cement floor, on top of cushions taken from the couch. The woman appeared skeletal and could hardly move or speak. Her grandmother, who brought her to the house along with her daughter, greeted us and expressed gratitude to have visitors. Evelyn and Mary gave the family blankets and hats, which people use even in almost 90-degree temperatures. The ladies also gave food that proved helpful for people limited by finances and mobility.

Mary and Evelyn also exercised a level of healthcare training recognized by the government. During every home visit they went through a chart providing the schedule of medications taken by the people. The medications provided very basic relief for pain, comfort for stomach issues, moisturizer for drying skin, etc. In every visit, Evelyn and Mary held people's hands, hugged them, and in some cases bathed them. Each act demonstrated a sense of solidarity with people who were going through a very difficult process. As we drove along, I asked Evelyn and Mary if they ever feared contracting sickness or diseases through contact with people. Evelyn laughed at me and just said, "and what would that matter, we still have to do what Jesus told us to do." I cannot help but think that Evelyn's and Mary's attitude didn't represent an abnormal identity for Christians. An attitude toward self-preservation and hoarding resources depicted abnormality. Evelyn and Mary simply lived out their Christian identity.

One also sees this Christian identity in an interesting piece from the second century. The following account originates from Eusebius, (circa 263 AD) and describes martyrs who died in the great pestilence in Alexandria:

> A violent pestilence laid waste the greatest part of the Roman Empire during twelve years, from 249 to 263. Five thousand persons died of it if one day in Rome, in 262. St. Dionysius of Alexandria relates, that a cruel sedition and civil war had filled that city with murders and tumults; so that it was safer to travel from the eastern to the western parts of the then known world, than to go from one street of Alexandria to another . . . there was not a single house in that great city which entirely escaped it, or which had not some dead to mourn for . . . The fear of death rendered the heathens cruel towards their nearest relations. As soon as any of them had caught the contagion, though their dearest friends, they avoided and fled from them as their greatest enemies . . . This sickness, which was the greatest of calamities to the pagans, was but an exercise and trial to the Christians, who showed, on that occasion, how contrary the spirit of charity is to the interestedness of self-love . . . in the time of this public calamity, most of them, regardless of the danger of their own lives in assisting others, visited, relieved, and attended the sick, and comforted the dying. They closed their eyes, carried them on their shoulders, laid them out, washed their bodies, and decently interred them, and soon after shared the same fate themselves.[4]

Our Christian identity does not necessarily include the ability to "helicopter in" and fix all of the problems around us. However, we see true Christian identity in Christian brothers and sisters such as Evelyn and Mary. They represent the incarnational presence of Christ that chooses to bear one another's burden intentionally.

A Christian identity of incarnational mission proves challenging within a pervasive short-term mission mindset. John 1: 14 asserts, "the word became flesh and dwelt among us." Phil. 2

---

4. Alban Butler, *The Lives of the Fathers, Martyrs and Other Principal Saints*

says that we should have the same mind in us which was in Christ Jesus who although he was God, he humbled himself and became obedient even unto death on the cross. At best, we truly cannot fix all of the sufferings around us, and perhaps that isn't our calling. We can, however, come alongside people such as Evelyn and Mary as, together, we live into the mission of God. More importantly we have to ask difficult questions about God's mission for us to our own hometown. Such living may occur at our own risk. In doing so, we live into our Christian identity. In this sense one cannot limit mission to a geographical location or program, rather mission becomes the nature of the Christian Church.

A MISSIONARY IDENTITY

South African missiologist David Bosch states, "Christianity has never been more itself, more consistent with Jesus and more evidently en route to its own future, than in the launching of world mission."[5] Mission, however, does not define a program of the church that originates in one part of the world and sent to another region. Mission does not serve as just another option for the church of Africa, Latin America, Haiti or anywhere else. The false idea that Europeans and North Americans exclusively "own" missions remains one of the greatest misunderstandings within colonialist periods of mission history. This mistaken notion leads many Christians in non-North American/European areas to think they can only receive the benefits of missions. Earlier in the book I provided an example of congregations from very different cultures finding a common mission. The congregation in Nairobi, Kenya partnered with the congregation in Kansas City, Missouri to live into their mission identity together. The congregation in Kansas City did not simply provide assistance to the congregation in Nairobi. Rather, both congregations choose to be missionary together. As they collaborate they combine cultural, personnel and financial resources in order to serve in a third location. An important

5. Bosch, *Transforming Mission: Paradigm Shifts in Theology of Mission*, 16.

understanding of mission emerges that geography does not limit mission practice. Those with financial resources do not reserve the right to originate a mission project. Nor does crossing salt water define mission activity.

Mission provides the very fabric of Christian identity. Without mission, the church is not the body of Christ. Missiologist Andrew Kirk observes, "The Church is by nature missionary to the extent that, if it ceases to be missionary, it has not just failed in one of its tasks, it has ceased being Church."[6] In this sense, therefore, God is a missionary God, and as the church reflects God's mission nature, the church is renewed in God's triune image.

THE CHURCH AS MISSIONARY

A vital aspect of healthy congregational partnerships, therefore, includes their focus on God's mission as an integral part of the church. Missions do not reflect solely a program that includes activities of doing good for those in far off countries. Nor does mission merely provide an opportunity for a cross-cultural experience. Instead of a singular idea that a sending church sends and supports those called to be missionaries. Or the counter idea that the church remains preoccupied with self-preservation. The church should identify itself as a "sending-sent" church. The sending-sent assumes a focus on God's missionary nature, so one does not limit mission to taking a trip or supporting a program. Instead, mission defines what the church does throughout the year. Pope Francis 2014 address to the catholic bishops and clergy states this sentiment. Francis speaks of the need to put all things in a "missionary key." He states,

> I dream of a 'missionary option,' that is, a missionary impulse capable of transforming everything, so that the Church's customs, ways of doing things, times and schedules, language and structures can be suitably channeled

6. Kirk, *What is Mission?*, 30.

for the evangelization of today's world rather than for her self-preservation."[7]

A major shift happens in a congregation that goes beyond one-directional, short-term, mission trips. Instead, a congregation works toward healthy practices of integrated congregational mission. The shift occurs not only when a church moves away from serial mission trips to a single location. Rather, the church moves toward healthy partnerships integrated into every aspect of the congregation. A move such as this appears possible when reciprocity allows for both partners to both learn from one another and to strengthen one another as co-workers in a common mission. It implies mutuality and mission practices that serve more than a trip or experience. Beyond mutuality, a transformation occurs in congregations that move beyond self-preservation. Instead, the church moves toward an understanding of mission as the church's primary identity rather than an organizational strategy. This shift, therefore, doesn't occur through implementing a program. The shift occurs by fostering a theological or ecclesiological understanding of the nature of the Christian church. One can discover through all of scripture an understanding of the Church as missionary, reflecting the very nature of God as a missionary God. One finds a resurgence of this perspective in ecumenical mission councils throughout the 20th century.

Ecumenical mission councils included a broad theological spectrum of Christian mission thinkers that wrestled with key concepts and practices for mission. One of the ongoing debates of the councils represented two very different perspectives of the church. Some proposed that the church should focus on its central identity as evangelization. The church should practice and think of mission as a utilitarian program designed to build the organization of the church. The utilitarian perspective surfaced in the church growth writings of authors such as Donald McGavern. These authors stressed the need for numeric growth through the use of strategic methods. On the other side of this discussion missiologists like Latin American missiologists Rene Padilla and Samuel Escobar

7. Pope Francis, Evangelii Gaudium, p. 25 paragraph 27

argued mission should be holistic in nature, not managerial or utilitarian. Lesslie Newbigin and David Bosch offered proposals emphasizing a missional theology that appeared similar to the *"mision integral"* theology of Padilla and Escobar. Newbigin served as a missionary to India until his retirement. When he returned home to England, he found a great need for mission to go beyond programs of simply sending people to serve in distant lands. He discovered a great need for mission that engaged western society as much as it did in distant lands.

In his book, *The Open Secret*, Lesslie Newbigin developed a missionary ecclesiology (the church as missionary) out of a Trinitarian approach to missions. Newbigin understood that a Trinitarian approach would set the work of the Trinity, instead of the Church, as the primary agent of mission. Newbigin argued,

> (A) Trinitarian approach to mission holds together three facets of the work of God in a dynamic and creative tension: the 'proclamation' of the Kingdom (in the authority of the Father), the 'presence' of the Kingdom (in and through the Son), and the 'prevenience' of the Kingdom (through the ministry of the Spirit who 'goes before' the Church in its missionary work)[8]

Newbigin's approach represented an understanding that would do justice to what the Bible said related to God's Mission.

A core Trinitarian understanding of mission appeared not particularly new in Newbigin. South African missiologist David Bosch built on the ecclesiology of Karl Barth in a more explicit way than Newbigin. Bosch arrived at many of the same conclusions that mission does not define an activity of the church, but rather reflects the very nature of the Triune God manifested in the church.[9] Church and mission represented interdependent elements in Bosch as well as Newbigin. One clearly sees the interdependence reflected in the words of David Bosch;

8. Newbigin, *The Open Secret*, 72.
9. Bosch, *Transforming Mission*, 373-380.

> It has become impossible to talk about the church with-
> out at the same time talking about mission. One can no
> longer talk about church *and* mission, only about the
> mission *of* the church . . . A church without mission or a
> mission without church are both contradictions.[10]

Missions, according to Bosch, remained "the church-with-others."[11]

In the New Testament, the Church sent apostles to people
of varied ethnic groups. The church, however, did not limit mission to merely sending missionaries to "the ends of the earth." As
the body of Christ reflected Gods nature of mission, the church
didn't retain missionaries. The church herself served as missionary
in Jerusalem, Judea, and Samaria . . . as well as to the ends of the
earth (Acts 1:8).

Another way to state this perspective asserts that the church
does not serve as merely a sending church; rather, it embodies a
"sent" church. Furthermore, a robust and perhaps more accurate
perspective would describe the church as a "sending-sent church."
David Bosch argues we must abandon the distinction between
"sending" and "receiving" churches and favor mutuality over hi-
erarchy. Bosch does not place emphasis on church as "location" or
"organization." Rather the church embodies a people who reflect
the mission nature of God. The church serves in relationship with
God, with one another, and with all of God's creation. This focus
reflects an integration of ecclesiology and mission.

Missional ecclesiology (the church as missionary) reflects
an emerging renewal of an ancient perspective of mission. Still,
the predominant paradigm in current evangelical missions entails
"supporting missions" instead of "being mission." The model of
a supporting church and sending church remain dominant in
many parts of evangelical missions. However, various congregational partnerships emerge based on collective or joint actions;
actions that enhance the effectiveness of all parties involved. In
this sense, a missiological shift appears to be emerging in congregational mission that reflects a move toward finding healthy

10 ,Ibid 372.

11. Ibid., 66.

principles of interdependence or networking relationships between congregations.

Ethnographic studies of congregational mission rarely indicate explicit connections between a missionary ecclesiology and congregational mission. Still one can discover a direct connection between congregations and individuals that see themselves as the participants in mission. These connections appear both in large-scale movements of short-term and congregational mission. As argued later on in this chapter, however, the connection proves incomplete without more explicit practices that connect global activity with day-to-day living.

Healthy congregational partnerships go beyond thinking of mission as a short-term trip, limited to a program to support, or the activity of a select few. Healthy congregational partnerships understand that mission remains a vital part of their identity as the body of Christ. This shift of perspective means that one cannot limit missions by borders, by church walls, or by finances. The church, by its very nature, is mission or missionary.

PRACTICAL IMPLICATIONS OF A MISSIONARY ECCLESIOLOGY

Congregational partnerships offer an opportunity for the church to find a practical expression of the theological framework just described. A word of caution, however, remains necessary at this point. The fact that a congregation possesses programs that involve mission trips, or maintains a dynamic, on-going mission partnership, does not necessarily mean the congregation defines a missionary church. Likewise, one cannot exclude a small church that cannot afford multiple mission trips from being missional. The church goes beyond the addition of more activities as it transitions from a program minded structure to a missional identity that places God's mission at the center.

The unique role of the lead pastor

Lead pastors often serve as the primary protagonist in congregational partnerships. This role appears new for many pastors. Pastors seem accustomed to people within their congregation or staff
taking lead in short-term missions or mission fund raising events.
Until recently most pastors supported the cause of missions, but
very few took a leading role. In contrast, many interviewed pastors
initiated new partnerships and remain passionately active. This active role includes mentioning the partnership in sermons, visiting
the host partner, and promoting fundraising.

Within some of the largest congregations I have spoken with,
lead pastors described the shift that happened as they moved away
from a focus on just faith promise giving (a common form of congregations to raise financial support for missions), and short-term
missions, to focus on congregational partnerships. These churches
often assumed short-term missions as a side-program, one led by
individuals in the congregation with a niche group of participants.
Although these congregations participated in faith promise giving,
the pastors reported that it had lost its luster. The short-term mission groups seemed limited to youth or, in some cases, confined to
those with construction skills. Although the congregation prayed
for those who traveled, supported them financially, and heard a
report when they returned, pastors reported a limited impact. In
some cases, the pastor even felt these projects appeared counter-
productive to the focus of their church.

One pastor of a large congregation described the shift toward
partnerships in this way:

> The concept of faith promise had grown a little stale for
> us. When you just looked at the support that it was get-
> ting, it was almost all the involvement level was from our
> older members, very little from our younger members
> or folks who weren't connected so I knew that we were
> missing something. I also knew that the whole work and
> witness concept (a short-term mission program that
> focuses on construction) was losing energy and because
> work and witness was for somebody who maybe wanted

to swing a hammer and [the idea that]if you can build a building [then] you can come and help us. If not, thank you, but send money instead. The problem with that was only about 5 percent of our congregation had these skills and was willing to take two weeks of their vacation time to do something that they weren't good at. So we had this idea of how can we involve multiple generations and how can we include people with all life skills in missions.

Another pastor of a smaller congregation in Hingham, Massachusetts stated,

It was clear that such things as supporting our denomination mission fund (which we still pay in full each year), individual missionary support, etc. did not connect very well with most of the young adults in our church. We had Faith Promises, etc., but any lasting connection to what God was doing throughout the world generally left as soon as any special speaker did, despite being a small congregation with a higher ratio of missionary-connected families than most our size (we have three MKs and two former missionaries in our church of 70 or so active participants with 50-55 in regular worship attendance).

He continued by saying

What I sought in a partnership wasn't simply a means to connect long-term with a church outside of the US, but was also a means to invigorate our own understanding of mission here in Hingham. I began speaking about our need to see ourselves as missionaries. Our church sits in a wealthy suburban town and only a handful of our regular attenders actually live in Hingham. There seemed to be somewhat of a fear of interacting with our neighbors and reaching out to Hinghamites. Part of my hope in envisioning a partnership was that whatever the Spirit was doing elsewhere in the world might rub off on us as we partner such that the Lord would spur us on here in Hingham. Quite honestly, "partnership" literally appealed to me in that I saw that we had resources (mostly money) that could benefit a church outside the US while

we had a need (mostly spirit and Spirit) that a church
outside the US could challenge us on.

Lead pastors demonstrated similar expressions in nearly all of the
studied partnerships. In some cases, people in the congregation
maintained connections to locations that directed the partnerships
to a specific place. In nearly all of the partnerships, however, the
lead pastor expressed a desire to be actively involved in the partnership as a way to renew his or her congregation's mission focus.

This active involvement proved very different from short-
term mission (STM) efforts, or mission giving programs like faith
promise. STM programs often included limited involvement from
the lead pastor since people in the congregation lead the efforts.
Furthermore, STM involved a limited group within the church.
Conversely congregational partnerships in this study demonstrated that an active involvement of the lead pastor engages the entire
congregation in missions.

One should note the shift toward the lead-pastor as the primary
advocate potentially produces challenges when the church changes
pastors. A couple of congregations surveyed, underwent pastoral
change during the time of their partnership. In these congregations,
the partnership did not end. In addition, the partnership seems to
continue without major problems. Perhaps the greatest challenge for
new lead pastors, with limited background, lies in understanding
how these partnerships fit within the church structure.

A broader understanding of mission

Most of the surveyed churches demonstrated substantial preparation for mission trips before people traveled. Some of them
began preparation a year before they left as people began to read
and learn about the country that they were going to visit. When
groups included people who had gone on previous trips, the new
participants learned from their veteran experience. In one case,
the church prepared a CD with key phrases in the language of the
host partner slowly enunciated by missionaries or people from the

country of their partnership. The CD also included the names of leaders team members might meet with a brief description of their role in the host partner location. In monthly meetings, team members would practice the phrases on the CD. Unlike the short-term mission teams described in other research projects, the partnerships surveyed maintained substantial preparations before leaving.

Post-trip follow up received less emphasis. Such efforts assisted team members to bridge their experiences in the host country to their experiences in the U.S. The post-trip follow-up in many churches included one or two group meetings that focused on the exchange of pictures and stories from the trip. A couple of churches offered an optional Sunday school class to discuss the implications of the trip.

I asked participants how the trip affected them when they returned, the responses varied. Discussions about dealing with poverty seemed common to most responses. On one extreme some individuals reported the experience made them antagonistic to people in poverty in the U.S. The following response by an individual interviewed shortly after return to the U.S. from Africa provides a representative example:

> One thing that I observed is you're in the USA, and you see this entitlement mentality, you owe me this . . . everything you hear is entitlement. Well, went there [Africa] and here are people who are poor, that are carrying their water, that have a bathroom that's a cement pipe in the ground and a solar battery to charge, a solar charger for their car battery so they can listen to the radio at night, no running water, no lights, they don't feel entitled to anything, ya know, you're not, they're not expecting you . . . like we owe them anything. It's like wow, you're here. Ya know, you came, they just were overwhelmed by the fact that people from the USA from outside of Africa cared to come there with no strings attached.

Most responses expressed confusion when, returning to the U.S., participants tried to process the financial disparity between the U.S. and majority world locations. People struggled finding ways to address these issues in the U.S. Most participants stated this feeling subsided after a couple of months. They returned to life as it was before. In some cases, participants found ways to contribute to the host partner. Only a handful of people interviewed connected the mission trip and local ministry to people in poverty, or from a different ethnicity.

Overwhelmingly, participants stated people longed to return to the host country. The perception surfaced that the greatest need, as well as the greatest personal fulfillment, occurred through serving in the host location. One participant noted:

> (Y)our mindset is so easily turned to God and to serving and it is so easy to fall into that and then you come here and there's just so many distractions, and to be honest it was hard to not look around and not be like, you guys have no idea, ya know? Like I mean we're just so spoiled . . . it was really hard, switching between the cultures and there's such an extreme so it was difficult.

> When you're there you're in an intergenerational community that is serving Christ together, it's really fantastic . . . it's just the ideal life. If it could be like that every day I would be much happier for sure.

> I really couldn't imagine going a year without doing a mission trip now. At least one or two a year. Financially they are taxing and you do have to get sponsorship but I can't imagine where my life would be if I decided that I'm not going to care about the rest of the world anymore.

> . . . it took me almost a month to plug back in. I felt spoiled rotten to the point it made me sick. I mean, I couldn't, it was like going through a drive through and getting something to eat just breaks your heart. Getting up out of our bed and knowing your toilet is right there, man, it breaks your heart. Just seeing that everything is so much easier here.

All in all, most people's experience of traveling to work with their host partner helped participants discover ways to be involved in ministry in the host location. The involvement included using their skills in medicine, business, construction, and especially in raising support. During the interview process, people emotionally described the renewal that happened in their own lives as well as in their congregation. A successful medical professional in his late 50's stated, "I felt that all of the experiences of my life came together and had meaning through my involvement in Swaziland." In one interview I asked the informant what the church gains by this partnership relationship. He responded "our salvation." He went on to state he didn't mean congregants were working for their salvation. Rather this activity in missions helps their church live out their true salvation.

SOME BEST PRACTICES FOR THE MISSIONARY CHURCH

The role of the lead pastor remains vital to healthy and holistic partnerships. The lead pastor represents the whole congregation and can explicitly help the congregation understand the connection between mission trips and mission living. This understanding occurs as the church comes together to worship as the gathered community, and then moves into the world as the sent community.

1. The mission pastor or coordinator, as a ministry role, also proves vital to healthy and holistic partnerships. In most congregations, the mission pastor saw their role as the networker or the organizer of the partnership as well as a minister within the congregation. This dual role appears important. The ministerial role helps the congregation to connect the mission trip to a broader perspective of God's mission in their work, their communities, and the places where they spend most of their time. The mission pastor should possess a broader ministry beyond the logistics of mission trips.

2. Practitioners should strongly emphasize follow-up activities alongside pre-trip activities. This addition helps people work through issues such as poverty and human suffering as global problems that occur in Africa as well as the U.S. Follow up activities should help participants who go on a trip to begin connecting what they learned on the trip to their daily lives.

The activities could include discussions of intentionally adjusting personal finances, as well as understanding and working to address local poverty, which may look very different than poverty in Africa. Activities might also address issues such as gender-based violence that happens either in other countries or within every community of the U.S.

As the church lives into mission as its primary identity, congregations provide a credible witness in the midst of a skeptical generation. That witness proves crucial to a people who lost confidence in a previous view of missions as primarily programs and unfortunate colonialist activities. Yet, when congregations renew the biblical and ancient practice of Christian mission, they unveil the authentic nature of the Church.

6

Collective Impact

"Big breakthroughs happen when what is suddenly possible meets what is desperately necessary"

—THOMAS FRIEDMAN, "COME THE REVOLUTION"[1]

"Though one may be overpowered, two can defend themselves. A cord of three strands is not quickly broken."

—ECCLESIASTES 4:12

A FIFTH PATTERN FOR healthy partnerships entails working with a platform organization for coordination. Amongst partnerships addressing complex global issues, those that thrived with the strongest potential for long-term impact remained connected to a larger platform organization.

---

1. Friedman, "Come the Revolution" *NYTimes, May 15, 2012*

WHEN THE IMPOSSIBLE BECOMES POSSIBLE

Participants often think of partnerships in terms of the congregation with resources working together with another congregation or area in need. The need may involve building buildings, perhaps installing water wells, assisting in evangelization, or completing other very definable objectives. In this sense, the projects seem very similar, if not the same, as those of serial short-term missions. Most congregations I surveyed exhibited a mixture of partnership patterns, but these activities seemed to dominate nearly all projects.

What if, however, the need and the objective of the partnership prove so large that it appears impossible for a single congregation, no matter how large, to address the problem? What if the partnership focused on turning the tide of HIV/AIDs in the most affected country, in the world? What if the partnership sought to make real change in gender based violence, human trafficking, drought, or similar issues?

Governments, wealthy individuals, and organizations have tried, with little success, to address similar issues layered with complexity. How does a congregational partnership realistically engage in such audacious endeavors? This final pattern for healthy partnerships reflects a focus on the *misio Dei*, the mission of God, which goes far beyond what people previously dreamed possible. This pattern focuses on the possibilities the church, as the body of Christ, possesses as a catalyst in addressing injustices and bringing holistic healing. Challenges that previously appeared elusive to government and relief organizations.

This chapter introduces collective impact as an approach for congregations that leverage resources and momentum as they make a genuine difference in issues such as HIV/AIDS, gender based violence, drought and other problems formerly thought "out of the reach" for the church. Collective Impact surfaces first through a story of a partnership in Swaziland that resulted in grants and donations totaling more than 50 million dollars for water wells. The chapter describes collective impact and compares the idea to isolated impact efforts that seem common to mission practice.

The writing then moves to describing platform organizations that serve as a type of cultural broker for large-scale efforts, facilitating collective impact. More than any other chapter, this chapter presents a means for the church to embody a credible witness in the midst of current global challenges. Collective impact in this chapter is applied to large congregations that address enormous global issues. The principles of strategic collaboration, however, are applicable to smaller congregations as well.

WINDMILLS AND WATER FOR A NATION

In chapter one of this book, I told the story of the Swaziland/ Bethany First Church partnership. How the partners made it their objective to drastically reduce HIV/AIDS in Swaziland, the most affected country in the world. Fred, whose story I referenced, served as part of a team from this congregation. Fred, and his wife Kathy, sat in the Sunday service when the pastor first presented the Swaziland Partnership to their church. Fred worked as an engineer installing oxygen and gas lines in hospitals in Oklahoma. Fred's highly specialized role in hospitals placed him in contact with many health professionals. Fred and Kathy served on the first team from BFC that went to *Sitsatsawani*, Swaziland where the church planned on building housing for nurses in a rural clinic. Fred described this clinic as:

> The worst clinic they had. It was so barren, and it was the middle of summer and there's not one green thing anywhere. The animals were dying, and they had no water. They have no clean water for an entire community of like 10,000 people. I don't know if you've seen dances with wolves where he goes out to that one army post that has just been abandoned. That's *Sitsatsawani*. They couldn't get nurses there to go and live because there's no nurse's housing. The nurses had to live in literally a corner of the clinic, couldn't even bring, (and it was a male nurse) couldn't bring his family from Mozambique, he was living on a cot on the floor, no running water, not one of these 17 clinics had any running water. They

were trucking it in and so that whole community was
dying, and I remember it when we came, we worked
on their church, and we started building a nurses
housing center.

As the team worked at a church in this community, Fred noticed a
school nearby which had an old windmill to one side. Fred started
asking about the windmill. Residents told him the windmill had
been out of service for years.

Fred started spending time in the evening at the windmill
and, as an engineer, he said, "I believe there's water in there, I know
we can get water out of that well. We just have to figure out how to
make it work." Fred went to a nearby water pump company where
he inquired about parts to repair the windmill, and he started to
build a friendship with the owner.

James Braithwaite a South African, owned the pump company. When interviewed, he stated Fred came knocking at the door of
his business, saying he was with a church group and wanted to talk
with him about installing a water well. Braithwaite's first inclination
was just shut the door and say "go away." Braithwaite reported he
tired of government and relief organizations that were "concerned
about their own benefit more than the benefit of the community."
According to Braithwaite, church groups seemed no different than
the government organizations. Both appeared more concerned
with short-term, status seeking, flash than with long-term benefit
for the community. As a result, participants installed water wells
that worked well for one to two years. However, the wells eventu-
ally broke down since they used cheap parts and were dependent
on electricity. Otherwise, vandals stole essential parts, making the
pumps useless to the community. However, Fred convinced Braithwaite, at least to listen to his proposal and give Fred advice.

Fred and Jimmy thought a solar paneled water system would
incur a long life span without depending on electricity. Furthermore, their water system required minimal maintenance. Pictures
that Fred brought to our Oklahoma City interview showed a rusty
inoperative windmill in a dry, desolate area. The pictures also revealed a team from the congregation circled around that windmill

praying that God would give needed water for the community. Fred returned home and began to collect funds to install a $20,000 solar paneled water pump in Sitsatsawani. Fred brought one last set of pictures to the interview, which he described with emotion. The pictures depicted children in Sitsatsaweni with water running down their chin as they got a drink from the newly installed solar powered water well.

I also interviewed Jim Copple about the water wells. At the beginning of this partnership Jim held no connection with BFC other than involvement in the same denomination as a child through early adulthood. He became active working with the U.S. government. He married a woman who was a successful Mormon grant writer in Salt Lake City, Utah. At the same time that Fred was in Swaziland, Jim, served as the co-director of an organization whose work involved brokering, facilitating, and mediating between various collaborators to achieve a common objective. Jim was also working in another African country on a grant through Coca Cola to install water wells.[2]

Jim reported that Coca-Cola, at this point, had already agreed to fund a water initiative in Swaziland. The low maintenance, solar paneled system of Jimmy and Fred at Sitsatsweni, however, impressed Coca-Cola. The system became a template for installing many similar systems throughout Swaziland. Coca Cola approached Braithwaite about his pump company to ask if the company could handle the contract without involving the church. Braithwaite, who had no connection with BFC or any church prior to this time, insisted these wells be connected to the church. The rationale included the church's infrastructure of medical clinics and schools throughout Swaziland. Braithwaite's experience indicated the church would serve the community in ways that proved essential for the wells to make a real impact.

The Sitsatsweni story recounts where the initiative of BFC, together with Jimmy and Fred's ingenuity, provided the basis for Jim to leverage a multi-million-dollar grant, benefiting many people throughout Swaziland. This same solar powered water well concept

2. See http://www.sai-dc.com/

indirectly influenced additional funding. Coca-Cola Africa Foundation provided $30 million, and USAID $23 million, in matching funds to develop similar water systems throughout the continent of Africa. This project received recognition through the Energy Global World Award in 2012.[3] Since AIDS lowers the immune systems of those infected, a clean water supply provides a major contribution to address HIV/AIDS in countries such as Swaziland.

Many of the water systems primarily connect to clinics. Clinics also link to churches and schools. These connections provide linked social capital for congregations. Congregations gain credibility as others implicitly connect the church's receiving grants to providing water for their communities.

Fred's part in this effort remains critical. However, the impact of the ministry went far beyond what Fred could ever do within his own ingenuity or fund raising ability. In describing this phenomenon of churches finding ways to address large-scale global issues, one must say that God adds an immeasurable part to the equation. God provides a grace that surpasses any strategic planning. Christians who understand their work as part of God's mission, God's grace, undergirds any strategy of healthy practices and focused effort.

COLLECTIVE IMPACT AND CONGREGATIONAL PARTNERSHIPS

The term Collective Impact describes cross-sector philanthropic efforts addressing large social issues in the U.S. Theorists do not specifically use the term to address religious humanitarian work, or international congregational partnerships. I am using the general concept of collective impact theory as a framework for describing the structure developed by the Swaziland Partnership.[4] I am also using this concept to encourage other congregations

3. See http://www.infrastructurene.ws/2012/06/13/swaziland-rain-project-garners-global-recognition/ and http://www.observer.org.sz/index.php?news=39744

4. Wesley, "Collective Impact in Mission" *Didache: Faithful Teaching*

toward similar partnership efforts, providing a framework for greater impact. This engagement represents an emerging form of missions described by missiologist Robert Priest. The movement supports Christians and churches that do not have resources alone to address this level of poverty and social challenge.[5]

The essence of collective impact theory asserts that large-scale social change requires broad cross-sector coordination, rather than the isolated intervention of individual organizations[6]. Similarly, collective impact addresses mission efforts that respond to systemic and large-scale problems such as the HIV/AIDS crisis in Swaziland. Problems participants cannot adequately address through smaller, individual, mission organizations, or through isolated efforts within a larger mission organization.

In missions, collective impact strategies network the congregation to multiple organizations. This network provides resources as the church attempts to address effectively an enormous global crisis such as HIV/AIDS. The concept of collective impact represents an approach where various organizations make a greater impact than the sum of the work they could individually accomplish as isolated organizations. Collective impact defines more than organizational collaboration. The concept reflects an intentional and disciplined approach to achieving large -scale impact beyond the capacity of any of the individual collaborators. Collective impact proves catalytic in forming a powerful, holistic response to complex issues.

Collective Impact theory, described by Kania and Kramer, entails an argument against isolated approaches within single organizations finding and funding solutions. The theory resists any result where independent organization invents independent solutions. The theory opposes competitive practices between organizations seeking to address the same issues. Findings in the Swaziland/BFC Partnership and other partnerships include elements of isolated impact in mission. However, they also include elements described as collective impact.

5. Priest, *A New Era of Mission is Upon Us.*
6. Kania, Collective Impact.

Theorists might easily describe the mission structure of many denominations and mission agencies as singular or isolated. Often these agencies work to benefit the organization directly, engaging activities compatible with the growth and doctrine of the denomination or organization. In this approach, one finds a strong focus on fundraising by congregations to support the mission efforts of the denominational mission agency. The following diagram illustrates prior efforts in the Swaziland partnership:

FIGURE 6: ISOLATED IMPACT IN SWAZILAND

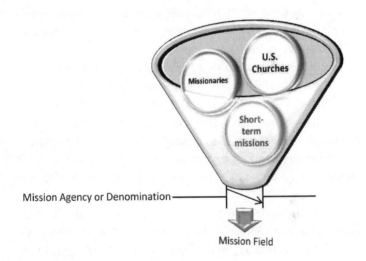

This figure represents a model in which mission related ministries of congregations, missionaries, and short-term mission, support the strategy and structure of the mission agency. Collectively they channel volunteer missions through the Global Mission denominational structure. The diagram represents Global Mission in the Africa Region.[7] The region serves as a valve in the funnel, one that provides both a safeguard and control for mission activities within

7. The Africa Region in the Church of the Nazarene is the denomination's administrative structure for the continent of Africa.

Swaziland. Historically this model worked well for congregations, the denomination, and the mission field. However, as grassroots efforts increase, such as short-term missions, large congregations with resources enter into partnerships directly with pastors and local leaders. Unfortunately, while partnering congregations need direction, the isolated impact structure of mission agencies may prove cumbersome for many of these congregations.

When strategists apply an isolated impact model to third wave mission movements, such as short-term mission or partnerships, they see other agendas surface. Guiding concerns appear whether the initiative contributes directly to the numeric growth of churches, and whether the initiative remains doctrinally consistent with the denomination or agency. An isolated impact system assumes that a central administrative system approves and channels ministries on the mission field.

Another form of isolated impact emerges from silo mission efforts, such as compassionate ministries, education, Jesus Film, or medical missions. Unfortunately, any one of these ministries may remain an isolated system with little or no cross sector organization. Denominational mission efforts sometimes provide another example, when participants work in isolation while attempting to address similar issues in the same area as other mission organizations.

Isolated impact may occur for good reason as opposed to a collective impact approach, whether based on historical or current conditions. The isolated impact model's strength emerges as long-term missionaries guide projects based on the mission organization's specific agenda. These missionaries bring specific, cultural sensitive, expertise that addresses issues such as dependency and healthy mission practices. The organization oversees projects in order to establish theologically and biblically consistent mission objectives and to build on lessons learned in the past.

Isolated impact defines the paradigm of mission most common in denominational structures. Arguably the paradigm provided a good platform for the expansive church growth around the world. The following chart provides a comparison of the two models:

ISOLATED IMPACT VS. COLLECTIVE IMPACT MODELS

Isolated Impact / Single System	Collective Impact / System of Systems
The mission agency seeks funding from congregations and donors to support specific programs. These programs offer solutions to strategies such as church development and evangelism.	The mission agency serves as a strategic partner which networks congregations and organizations in diverse locations and also serves as a cultural and strategy liaison.
Organizations such as denominations and specific ministries work separately and compete to produce the greatest independent impact.	Effectiveness is measured by working toward common goals and measuring the same things.
Evaluation isolates a particular organization or ministries impact.	Large scale impact depends on increased cross-sector collaboration of multiple organizations.
Objectives of ministry are defined by mission specialists.	Objectives and agreed upon ministries are a collaborative effort which includes mission specialists as well as congregations, and multiple entities.

Instead of a single (or isolated) system approach, researchers might best describe the emerging collective impact model in partnerships (such as the Swaziland Partnership) as a system of systems. In the collective impact model multiple systems may still work independently. However, the places where activity converges across systems remain most important. Some agencies may prove stronger and more independent than other, interdependent, agencies. Significantly no one agency controls the activity. Rather common agreements provide strategic points of intersection. This partnership approach emerges not from higher levels of administration within the mission structure. Rather, based on common felt needs, a variety of organizations collaboratively address large issues (such as HIV/AIDS) that lie beyond the capabilities of one entity. The denomination or mission agency operates as a strategic partner in the system rather than the controlling agent.

This figure illustrates the emerging system of systems model of the Swaziland Partnership (or collective impact model):

FIGURE 7: COLLECTIVE IMPACT IN THE
SWAZILAND PARTNERSHIP

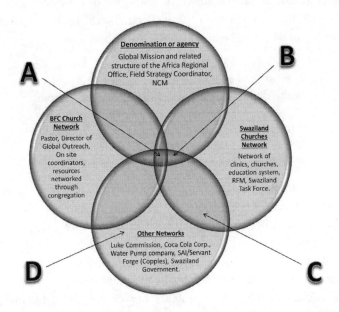

In this model, the collective impact with the greatest potential (point A) reflects the point of strongest connection or the greatest number of common networking. The other intersecting points (Points B and C) demonstrate a lesser degree of impact. Silo efforts (Point D) indicate even fewer results.

The Water Well initiative begun by BFC provided an example of a "point A" collective impact. (1) The BFC Network proved catalytic as one of their team members explored the need for a working water pump (an unplanned project). The member contacted a pumping contractor in Swaziland and raised $20,000 at BFC for the first water well. (2) BFC networked with an organization (SAI/Servant Forge) to leverage a multi-million dollar grant that would benefit many people throughout Swaziland. 3) The Swaziland Nazarene infrastructure provided an effective venue for connecting the water to communities through its 150 churches, 17 clinics, and 43 primary schools. 4) Nazarene Compassionate Ministries Inc. provided a system of accountability and sustainability through the Africa regional church structure. As noted, this project received recognition through the Energy Global World Award in 2012.[8] Beauty Makhubela, NCM director in Swaziland states,

> It [the water well initiative] is literally saving a generation from extinction because it has provided clean water to health clinics who can now initiate and sustain treatment for HIV/AIDS and TB, garden projects that feed HIV/AIDS support groups and orphans, and communities that now have an economic future because they have clean water.

If BFC and the Swaziland churches operated in isolation, the impact would have been drastically limited in comparison. According to James Braithwaite (the owner of Agro Pump company in Swaziland mentioned earlier), an initiative solely between Coca Cola and the Swazi Government lacked the necessary infrastructure. An infrastructure provided by the church.

The resulting project provides a qualitative, as well as quantitative, benefit. Beyond the immediate benefit, churches in Swaziland possess linking social capital. This capital allows them to carry forward their mission of evangelism and church growth. The collaborative approach, as opposed to an isolated approach, does risk a loss of mission focus on evangelism and church growth. However, Pastors and leaders interviewed in Swaziland state that this type of a joint effort gives the church greater credibility. This credibility results in greater evangelism and church growth.

An example of a Point B relationship rests with the Swaziland Task Force. The Swaziland Church Network serves as the primary element by establishing the strategy and initiative for the Task Force. In a limited manner, the South Africa and Swazi

---

8. See http://www.infrastructurene.ws/2012/06/13/swaziland-rain-project-garners-global-recognition/ and http://www.observer.org.sz/index.php?news=39744 (accessed January 20, 2012).

Governments provide aid. To a lesser degree Nazarene Compassionate Ministries and BFC remain involved.

The Luke Commission, a non-denominational mission organization in Swaziland, provides another example of a point B relationship. The Luke Commission maintains mobile medical clinics which utilize the Nazarene system of schools throughout the country. They also give space for medical doctors with BFC teams to work alongside them. The Luke Commission exhibits a form of collective impact independent of their involvement with Bethany First church. The intersection between BFC and the Luke Commission, therefore, represents two independent systems with a mutual point of interest.

Team members from BFC appear highly impacted by the Task Force as well as the Luke Commission. The Luke Commission receives donations of medical equipment such as a portable x-ray as team members return to the U.S. and connect their network of resource in the U.S. to the need in Swaziland. The Task Force exerts an emotional impact on team members and creating an impact for underserved communities.

The benefits of the Swaziland Partnership for the Task Force however remain limited. The limitation may be in part because their need requires ongoing subsidy, and they remain less dependent on equipment and U.S. connections than the Luke Commission. When guest churches primarily own both the concept and the implementation of projects, they limit creative input from host country or other organizations. Such projects also possess limited potential when compared to ones done in convergence with the other systems.

For participants on STM teams connected to partnerships, the expressed impact on them proves greater when they maintain stronger connections to multiple contacts as well. In the Swaziland Partnership, participants who remain part of large groups encountered a more isolated experience since most of their interaction was within group members. Additionally, those who go once seem less impacted than those participating regularly on smaller teams.

Participants on large teams (40+ members) stated the bonding with other team members appears great. However, they also voiced concern about the effectiveness of the home visits with the Task Force. Further, returning participants described reinforced cultural bias toward those of other ethnicities or socio-economic statuses in the U.S. Team participants reported more positive impact if they engaged with churches and organizations while on a small team in the host country. Participants who made multiple trips reported more positive results both on the trip and when they returned. Smaller, repeated, trips resulted in further volunteering and donations (primarily to Swaziland).

Isolated impact limits how single organizations, such as denominations and other Christian groups, make large-scale, lasting impact on their own. Participants realize that many problems (such as HIV/AIDS, human trafficking, etc.) prove more complex and too systemic for simple solutions . Many isolated attempts include large-scale, expensive efforts resulting in limited or negative results. Further research into collective impact models in mission may provide answers how the church works more interactively as a whole body.

The model of collective impact in mission described in this chapter provides a subject that warrants further research and intentional development. To date, most research in congregational partnerships focused on the work being done in isolated approaches between a congregation and a field. Emerging models of mission appear to move beyond isolated efforts on the part of congregations, mission agencies or denominations. These models present a challenge, as well as potential. They call the Church to be the Body of Christ in ways that demonstrate authentic witness in the face of global challenges.

PLATFORM ORGANIZATIONS

When congregational partnerships grow complex, such as those described in the previous section, a platform organization proves necessary and vital for collective impact. In fact, one might argue that this need unveils reasons for failed initiatives like Bruce Wilkinson mentioned previously. A platform organization works to assure healthy partnership practices. The organization establishes means of accountability, builds public will, bridges all entities and, in some cases, mobilizes funding.

In some surveyed partnerships, the platform organization surfaced as an established organization that maintained a presence in the location of the partnership. For some large congregations, the platform organization presented a challenge. At times, the organization viewed the partnership as a means to support their organization rather than facilitating the common mission between the guest and host congregations. In the Swaziland partnership, the platform organization both represented a foundation interested in addressing HIV/AIDS epidemic and maintained a vested interest in the congregation. This organization helped establish mutual agreements between those in Swaziland and the congregation. They wrote grants for initiatives and continued to network all of the entities involved.

7

A Common Mission

Brothers and sisters, I could not address you as people who live by the Spirit but as people who are still worldly—mere infants in Christ. ² I gave you milk, not solid food, for you were not yet ready for it. Indeed, you are still not ready. ³ You are still worldly. For since there is jealousy and quarreling among you, are you not worldly? Are you not acting like mere humans? ⁴ For when one says, "I follow Paul," and another, "I follow Apollos," are you not mere human beings?

⁵ What, after all, is Apollos? And what is Paul? Only servants, through whom you came to believe—as the Lord has assigned to each his task. ⁶ I planted the seed, Apollos watered it, but God has been making it grow. ⁷ So neither the one who plants nor the one who waters is anything, but only God, who makes things grow. ⁸ The one who plants and the one who waters have one purpose, and they will each be rewarded according to their own labor. ⁹ For we are co-workers in God's service.

—I CORINTHIANS 3

TWO PERSPECTIVES

As noted in chapter one, readers might understand the title for this book, *A Common Mission* from two perspectives. Both perspectives consistently inform healthy partnership practices. Readers should first understand that "common" mission demonstrates the sense that mission remains mutual, one shared equally by two or more participants. Consistent with healthy missiological practices, geography and resources do not limit equal participation in mission. Equal partnership reflects a common theme in the first century church. Mutuality includes other Christians. However, mission quality remains dependent upon God, the Author of our faith, the One who makes things grow. As Paul states in I Cor.3, "we are co-workers in God's service."

The concept of our common mutuality remains closely related to the church's understanding of the Trinity. Gregory of Nanzianzus, the fourth century archbishop of Constantinople and Trinitarian theologian, described the nature of the Trinity using the image of dance or *perichoresis*. This metaphor describes the Triune God *and* proves helpful in describing the nature of the body of Christ. *Perichoresis* suggests moving around, making room, relating to one another without losing, or taking, identity. At the heart of this description lies a mutuality and reciprocity among all parts. As the Trinitarian view of the nature of God revolves around mutuality and reciprocity, the same view must also describe the nature of the church as the body of Christ.

The second understanding of "common" mission includes the sense that mission provides a common aspect threaded through the whole Christian community. Mission does not describe a special or isolated part of the church. Mission, rather, defines a foundational or persistent property of the church, common to all Christian communities. Another way to state this belief asserts mission resides within the DNA of the Image of God, and weaves throughout the very fabric of God's creation. Therefore, denying the *missio Dei*, or God's mission, denies our core identity and God's creativity.

IMPLICATIONS OF THE BEST PRACTICES FOR HEALTHY PARTNERSHIPS

A reflective reader might simply ask, "so what?" How does this focus on mission, and the best practices for healthy partnerships, impact local congregations, mission agencies and denominations?

1. Perhaps the most challenging implication rests with the assertion that church and mission prove inseparable. In other words, every Christian church, no matter how small or how limited in resources, from its inception exudes mission by its very nature. Congregants cannot limit mission to evangelistic programs, geographical boundaries, or traditional forms. Mission, rather, exists as an expression of the church's identity, an evangelistic expression that crosses frontiers and goes to the ends of the earth. In our globalized context, however, mission also crosses neighborhood "frontiers" to the immigrants within our own communities. Mission expresses its Christian witness as congregations love those separated from the church by ethnicity, language, sexual orientation, religion, or fear.

   As resource-rich guest churches enter into partnership with resource-limited host congregations, the guest church should consider how their host partner already lives into God's mission. Lesslie Newbigin states "To condemn the indigenous churches to be mere receptacles for converts while the tasks of mission belong to another body is to do the gravest possible spiritual injury to the young church."[1] From the very beginning, healthy missiological practices lead newly formed congregations to understand that practicing Christianity remains synonymous with participation in mission. Christian participation intentionally results in the spread of the Gospel. Otherwise, lack of these practices may result in long-term damage. Churches cease to concern themselves with others in their community. Congregations seem

1. http://www.newbigin.net/assets/pdf/58obog.pdf Downloaded April 28, 2014.

concerned with only their own wellbeing while depending on others with resources to carry out mission.

As Lesslie Newbigin would baptize new believers in India he would say,

> Now you are the Body of Christ in this village. You are God's apostles here. Through you they are to be saved. I will be in touch with you, I will pray for you. I will visit you. If you want my help, I will try to help you. But you are now the Mission.[2]

This perspective provides enormous implications for congregations entering into global partnerships with other congregations. A guest congregation must realize that, although the host may possess limited resources, the host church does not represent a *tabula rasa* or blank slate. As participants realize even churches with limited resources remain called to mission, they accept that principles of reciprocity and mutuality prove key to a healthy relationship.

There are various ways a partnership can fan to flame the call to mission within every congregation. One way entails mission activities that involve the host and the guest congregation working together in a third location. This approach allows two congregations to serve as co-workers in a common mission. In some cases, the activity may stretch host congregations. Partnership may challenge host congregations that previously thought of mission as an activity for those from the west. Now host congregations may need to think beyond their previous assumptions. When a partnership primarily reflects a donor and a recipient mindset, participants find it challenging to maintain healthy partnership focused on mission. Common mission partnerships produce a reciprocal relationship instead of a dependent relationship.

Furthermore, this perspective does not exclude smaller churches from partnerships. When I began researching congregational partnerships, I assumed only larger churches

2. Ibid.

would be involved in partnerships. I sent my first survey to measure the scope of partnerships only to churches of 500 or more members. Without a doubt, large churches reflect a much higher percentage of partnerships. However, many smaller churches also find creative ways to join as a cluster of congregations or to develop other unique ways to engage in partnerships.

2. Although God calls every church to mission, global partnerships may not be the best option for some congregations. The current popularity of global partnerships encourages pastors and church leaders to find a church in a different world area and start a partnership. Before entering a long term commitment, however, care must be taken to:

   a. Assess your own congregation. Among the congregations surveyed, nearly all lead pastors gained assent from their church board, as well as their congregation, before moving forward. In some cases, this process took a year or more. The partnership will be limited if a pastor retains a passion for a partnership, but their church board and/or congregation do not share the passion, nor needed investment. In the case of Bethany First Church, the board remained adamant the partnership should not take the place of their support of their denominational mission giving. Rather, partnership giving would go beyond denominational support. This commitment meant the church would more than double their current mission giving. They would continue to give around $600,000 a year to their denomination's mission fund. The partnership funding would include giving above and beyond that baseline. As the pastor approached the congregation, he presented the need and the vision; as well as their commitment to continue supporting their denominational mission structure. The pastor did not ask for donations or decisions until more than three months later. The congregation could pray about whether they would enter the partnership. This partnership proved consuming for the church as well as the pastor. Five years into the partnership the pastor accepted and moved to a different assignment. However, since the partnership involves the whole congregation and board, it continues to support the denominational mission structure. As people become more actively involved, the church also continues to multiply its donations and support of Swaziland.

b. Assess whether the partnership is a good fit for your congregation. Every congregation has its own personality including a variety of skills and resources. In the same way, every host congregation must also consider its own personality in order to find a good match for both partners. Most congregations sent a search team to the host site to meet a potential partner, and to get a feel for the nature of the potential activities. The search team represented a key point in the life of any partnership. Just as pastors must obtain the assent of their church board and congregation, a vital assessment reveals both partners assenting to a mutual commitment in the partnership.

Congregations with a high percentage of medical professionals, such as Bethany First, find working in partnership with substantial medical needs a good fit. In other congregations that possess other skills or resources, participants find it wise to ascertain whether the resources and the needs remain compatible. Likewise, the resources of the host partner prove vital to a healthy partnership relationship. For example, the Kenya congregation maintained established ministries in rural areas needing water wells. These ministries provided an important resource for Jacob's Well church, which partnered with the Kenya church to install wells.

1. Take the necessary time to establish a healthy framework before sending large numbers of volunteers. Participants should design congregational partnerships for a long-term, effective ministry that impacts the guest congregation. The ministry should also establish healthy patterns in the host location,

moving toward sustainable models of ministry. The five patterns for healthy partnerships in this book require intentional and careful steps before the partnership begins. The healthy patterns also require on-going assessment that assumes the need for continual, quality communication throughout the life of the partnership. Practicing the patterns involves cross-cultural communication between the host and the guest partner. Clear communication should also happen within the congregations of each partner.

In some of the congregations surveyed, I discovered banners about the partnership throughout the church facility. Participants established websites dedicated to the partnership.[3] Participants prominently displayed both banners and posters about the partnership in Sunday School classes, and worship areas for children and youth. Participants highlighted periodic activities, such as 5k runs and dinners, to raise funds for the partnership. Adults, participating on teams to the partner site, often gave reports with pictures to the children. In addition, they presented information in the majority of worship services, including either a video, or an announcement, or a prayer request for the partnership. The participants' objectives included continually informing and involving the whole congregation through prayer and giving.

2. Congregational partnerships provide important implications for mission agencies and denominational mission programs. Within Schrieter's second wave of mission, congregations supported mission agencies and denominational mission programs by sending funds to the agency. The agency would then represent the congregation as it sent out missionaries. However, in the third wave of mission congregations now ask how the agency or denomination helps them realize their desire actively to engage in mission. Congregational partnerships represent a challenge as well as an opportunity for these organizations. The challenge includes finding new ways to

---

3. The following is an example: http://www.swazipartners.org/

work with congregations other than simply coercing them to fund missions. Leaders within denominational structures that traditionally train and prepare individual missionaries will need to use similar tools to train and equip congregations. The opportunity includes faithfully living into the intention of scripture. Living into scripture equips the whole church to serve as missionaries to the whole earth.

3. Congregational partnerships raise implications for the local church to consider carefully its own context. I have intentionally avoided the temptation to make this book simply a "how to" guidebook for partnerships since context informs practices. I included theological sections that point to the holistic aspects of mission. These sections point out that mission does not describe a trip or program of the church. One cannot reduce mission to any activity that happens as we get onto an airplane or cross a national border. Rather, mission must represent the heartbeat of any congregation. Mission transforms a congregation as it comes together for worship. Mission also leads the church to be transformative as it moves into its own community.

Practices that bring both congregational and contextual renewal do not happen simply because the churches engage in a partnership. The partnership, however, does provide a framework for guest congregations to reflect on their host partners, who may be living their faith in challenging and very different circumstances. Beyond this benefit, the partnership provides space for guest congregants returning from trips to reflect on their experience of unsettling things. The reflection may assist congregants intentionally find new ways to live into their faith.

People often express a desire for renewal within the church of North America. Renewal, however, will not automatically happen as we return to a model of the first century church. Neither will renewal occur through any simple return to another paradigm of earlier generations. Renewal comes, however, as the church lives into its ancient identity as the body of Christ within the 21st century context. As the global church finds ways to live into its common identity as the body of Christ, my prayer remains that God will renew us and breathe life through us into our broken global context.

Bibliography

Adeney, Miriam. *Daughters of Islam: Building Bridges with Muslim Women.* Downers Grove, Ill.: Intervarsity Press, 2002.

Ammerman, Nancy. *Pillars of faith: American Congregations and their Partners.* Berkeley: University of California Press, 2005.

Bosch, David Jacobus. *Transforming Mission: Paradigm Shifts in Theology of Mission: Paradigm Shifts in Theology of Mission.* Maryknoll, New York: Orbis Books, 1991.

Buber, Martin. *I and Thou.* Edinburgh: T. & T. Clark, 1937.

Butler, Alban. *The Lives of the Fathers, Martyrs and Other Principal Saints,* Vol. 1 New York: P. J. Kenedy, 1903, 482–483

Drucker, Peter and Peter Fernando Drucker. Post Capitalist Society. New York: Harper Collins, 1993.

Easterly, William. *The White Man's Burdon: Why the West's Efforts to Aid the Rest Have Done so Much Ill and so Little Good.* New York: Penguin, 2006.

Elmer, Duane. *Cross-Cultural Connections: Stepping Out and Fitting in Around the World.* Downers Grove, Ill.: Intervarsity Press, 2002.

Freidman, T. "Come the Revolution." *New York Times* May 15, 2012. Accessed July 16, 2014, http://www.nytimes.com/2012/05/16/opinion/friedman-come-the-revolution.html?_r=0

Francis I. *Apostalic Exhortation Evangelii Guadium of the Holy Father Francis To the Bishops, Clergy, Consecrated Persons and the Lay Faithful on the Proclamation of the Gospel in Today's World.* Vatican Press. Accessed May 5, 2014, http://w2.vatican.va/content/francesco/en/apost_exhortations/documents/papa-francesco_esortazione-ap_20131124_evangelii-gaudium.html

Gupta, Paul R. "What the Global Church Wants the West to Know about Partnership" (plenary address, COSIM conference, Orlando, Fla., June 20-22, 2005).

Hutnyk, John. *The Rumour of Calcutta: Tourism, Charity and the Poverty of Representation.* London: Zed Books, 1996.

Bibliography

Kania, John and Mark Kramer. "Collective Impact." *The Stanford Social Innovation Review* (2011): 36-41.

Kirk, Andrew J. *What is Mission: Theological Explorations.* Minneapolis: Fortress Press, 2000.

Lupton, Robert D. *Toxic Charity: How Churches and Charities Hurt Those They Help.* New York: Harper Collins, 2011.

Maranz, David E. *African Friends and Money Matters: Observations from Africa.* Dallas:SIL International, 2001.

McGavran, Donald Anderson. *Understanding Church Growth.* Grand Rapids, Mich.: Wm. B. Eerdmans Publishing Co, 1970.

McQuilkin, Robertson. "Stop Sending Money! Breaking the Cycle of Missions Dependency. *Christianity Today* (1999): 57-59.

Moyo, Dambisa. *Dead Aid: Why Aid is Not Working and How There is a Better Way for Africa.* New York: Farrar, Straus and Giroux, 2009.

King, Gordon W., et al. *Going Global: A Congregation's Introduction to Mission Beyond Our Borders.* St. Louis, Mo.: Chalice, 2011.

Nevius, John. *Planting and Developing of Missionary Churches.* 4th ed. Philipsburg, NJ: Presbyterian and Reformed, 1958.

Newbigin, Lesslie. *The Open Secret: An Introduction to the Theology of Mission.* Rev. ed. Grand Rapids, MI.: Eerdmans, 1995.

————. "Sign of the Kingdom." *Scottish Journal of Theology* 35, no. 05 (1982): 462-463.

Nussbaum, Barbara. "Ubuntu: Reflections of a South African on our Common Humanity." *Perspectives* 17, no. 1 (2003): 21-26.

Phillips, Michael. "Unanswered Prayers: In Swaziland, U.S. Preacher Sees His Dream Vanish." *Wall Street Journal* (2005), accessed May 5, 2014 http://online.wsj.com/news/articles/SB113495910699726095.

Priest, Kersten Bayt. *Caring for the Least of These: Christian Women's Short-Term Mission Travel.* PhD diss., Loyola University Chicago, 2009.

Priest, Robert J. 2007. "Peruvian Churches Acquire Linking Social Capital through Short-Term Mission Partnerships." *Special Issue on Short-Term Missions in Latin America. Journal of Latin American Theology: Reflections from the Global South* (2007) 175-189.

————. "A New Era of Mission is Upon Us." In *Evangelical and Frontier Mission: Perspectives on the Global Progress of the Gospel,* edited by Beth Snodderly and A. Scott Moreau, 294-304. Oxford: Oxford Centre for Mission Studies, 2011.

Putnam, Robert D. and David E. Campbell. *American grace: How religion divides and unites us.* New York: Simon & Schuster, 2010.

Schwartz, Glenn J. "Cutting the Apron Strings." *Evangelical Missions Quarterly,* no. 30 (1994): 36-43.

Spurgeon, Charles H. "A Sermon and a Reminiscence." *Sword and the Trowel* (1873), accessed May 1, 2014, http://spurgeon.org/s_and_t/srmn1873.htm.

Thomas, Philip H.E. "How can Western Christians Learn from Partners in the World Church?" *International Review of Missions* 92, no. 366 (2003): 381-394.

Volf, Mirsolav. *A Public Faith: How followers of Christ should serve the common good.* Grand Rapids: MI Brazos Press, 2011.

Wesley, D. "Collective Impact in Mission." Didache Faithful Teaching, 12:1 (Summer 2012), accessed June 14, 2014, http://didache.nazarene.org/index.php/volume-12-1/863-didache-v12n1-03-collective-impact-mission-wesley/file.

Wuthnow, Robert. "Religious Involvement and Status-Bridging Social Capital." *Journal for the the Scientific Study of Religion* 41 (2002): 669-84.

———. *Boundless Faith: The Global Outreach of American Churches.* Berkeley: University of California Press, 2009.

Yoshikawa, Muneo Jay. "The Double-Swing Model of Intercultural Communication between the East and the West." In *Communication Theory: Eastern and Western Perspectives,* edited by D. Lawrence Kincaid, 319-329. New York: Academic Press, 1987.

An Invitation to Partnership

I trust that this book has served its purpose as an initial description and interpretation of congregational partnerships.

In the spirit of A Common Mission you are invited to partner with me in an exercise of reciprocity. I will be having on-going conversations about congregational partnerships at http://partnership.globalnaz.org/ as well as my own blog site at commonmission.blogspot.com. Through these sites you can contribute to the on-going conversation about best practices in congregational partnerships. My goal is to use these sites to give further examples of developments in partnership, and a way to share resources from congregations, mission agencies, and from those conducting research. If you would like to communicate directly with the author, email dwesley@nts.edu

Grace and Peace to you as you continue to live into
the mission of God,

David Wesley